After the Loss of a Spouse

Henry VIII to Julia Child

Lisa Saunders

Front cover images:
King Henry VIII by Hans Holbein the Younger, Walker Art Gallery, Liverpool
Attribution: Workshop of Hans Holbein the Younger 1497/8 (German) Details of
artist on Google Art Project • Public domain. (Retrieved from
https://en.m.wikipedia.org/wiki/Henry_VIII_of_England#)

Julia Child. Citation: KUHT-TV (Television station: Houston, Tex.). *Julia Child,
Image 2*. 1953 - 2011. Special Collections, University of Houston Libraries.
University of Houston Digital Library. Web. May 24, 2016.
http://digital.lib.uh.edu/collection/p15195coll38/item/233.

Unless otherwise noted, images within the text are by Lisa Saunders

Published by Act II Publications, LLC
PO Box 752, East Lyme CT, 06333.
www.PathfinderMag.com
860-460-0248
JMoore@widowedpathfinder.com

DEDICATION

In memory of my dad,

Richard W. Avazian (1937 – 2015)

Dad loved proofreading my "Widow/ers of History" articles before I submitted them to the editor of *Pathfinder: A Companion Guide for the Widow/er's Journey* magazine. Several of the books in my bibliography are biographies he had given me over the years.

And to my mother, Mary Ann Avazian,

Who has just embarked on her own widow journey with great courage.

REVIEWS

"Lisa Saunders has written an indispensable book about life after loss—and what we can learn from history's famous (and occasionally infamous) widows and widowers. There's something to be said for the resilience of the human spirit, and this book is a testament to that."
— *John Valeri, Hartford Books Examiner*

"Lisa Saunders has written another fine piece of historically-based literature. Based on a unique and previously uncovered topic in history, this work encompasses a broad span of time and shows clearly the commonalities, as well as uniquenesses, of these stories about the famous. How they handled their loss, their guilt, and in some cases a plan for a future without their spouses, makes fascinating reading for anyone with interest in both the history and the human side of well-known figures."
— *David S. Martin, Professor/Dean Emeritus, Gallaudet University*

"Anyone who loves a romantic history lesson will be intrigued by this book. Stories of love and loss depict the most bittersweet of human experience.   "
— *Dr. Joanne Z. Moore, Publisher*

EPIGRAPH

A year before my dad died, when he had no idea his time was drawing near, he wrote the following poem to express his longing for friends and family who had left our world for the next:

A Walk Before Dawn
by
Richard W. Avazian

The familiar places no longer seem the same
As ghosts of the past exhort me to make them live again
But my voice is inaudible in the raucous present
And as I fear, the dawn chases these phantoms
Never to live again, except in fond remembrance

Just before Dad died of cancer on July 14, 2015, he told me he looked forward to seeing those who had passed on before him, but felt sad at the thought of how much he was going to miss us.

Until we meet again

FOREWORD

by
Dr. Joanne Z Moore

Too many good books end when one partner in a marriage or committed relationship dies. I've always wondered how the survivors managed for the rest of their lives. Lisa Saunders, my friend and history buff, explored this idea with insatiable curiosity. She chose both men and women. Many are quite famous and are well loved. Others may fall into the infamous category, but we are still intrigued. Even people with fame, power, and wealth experience all the emotions that are universally human. Lisa digs into the personal side of their lives, and teases out the stuff that really matters.

In these stories, we "try on" how other people have dealt with life after the loss of a spouse. How does being a recluse feel? How about donating millions to a school for needy boys? Maybe marrying a librarian? Or marrying a woman who wanted to be a nun? These and many more adventures are recounted in this book.

Storytelling is the art of sharing our human experiences. Listening to a story is a way of trying on another way of life for size. My favorite stories are those with rich characters, who fall in love and struggle through life together. Very often the books end with "they lived happily ever after." In fact, we heard that story ending so often, we took for granted that once we found our Prince Charming or Princess Perfect that we, too, would live happily ever after. We planned every detail of the wedding, invited our friends to surround us and shower us with gifts. Few people hear the part of the wedding vow, "'til death do you part." When we're young and in love, death seems an eternity away. So when the inevitable happens, we grieve, in shock, and without an idea of how to go on.

No one who is still married wants to think about this sort of thing. It's kind of depressing. I get it. But if you can get over that initial anxiety, I think you'll find that the stories are just plain interesting and entertaining. And someday, you might find it a little easier to talk with someone who is unwillingly single again. You'll have a frame of reference for a conversation.

The natural thing to do after a loss is to seek role models. How have the people we admire handled this stage of life? And maybe even, who has set a course for themselves that we do not admire? Of course we look to family members, neighbors, and friends. Even the funeral director guides us through many of the business related details. We share many modern stories in our magazine, *Pathfinder: A Companion Guide for the Widow/er's Journey*.

(See www.PathfinderMag.com).

We can learn, too, from those historical figures who have walked this path before us. After all, being widowed is nothing new. It's part of the human experience, and so through storytelling, we can get a glimpse into others' lives. We can compare and contrast how gender, culture, faith, fame, and era all influence how a person lives after loss. We can study their conflicts, and see how they made decisions. As much as anyone can, we try to understand their emotional journey. We can be entertained, uplifted, taught, and inspired.

This is a great book for anyone who has ever been in love. The age-old theme of love and loss is absolutely the bittersweet human condition.

Dr. Joanne Z. Moore, Publisher, Act II Publications, LLC
Joanne Z. Moore, PT, DHSc., OCS, is the owner of Shoreline Physical Therapy in East Lyme, Connecticut. She is the editor of the digital magazine, Pathfinder: A Companion Guide for the Widow/er's Journey, *and the author of the guidebook,* After the Loss of a Spouse: What's Next?

Lisa Saunders

Table of Contents

Lisa Saunders

PREFACE

I first became interested in life after the death of a spouse when I watched my grandmothers handle the shock of sudden widowhood—one grandfather died of a heart attack, the other in a farming accident. Both of my grandmothers were widowed in their 50s, both still had their health, and neither were financially secure.

One grandmother hadn't worked for years, didn't know how to balance a checkbook, and did little to improve her situation—other than complain about how little money she had. Visiting her, sad to say, became an obligation, not a joy.

My other grandmother did what she had to do to get on with her life. After some months of heavy grieving, she sold her farm and took a certification course in home health care. That eventually led to a full-time job in a nursing home—one that she loved. Not only did she entertain me with tender and humorous stories about the residents who became like family to her, but she fell in love with the janitor—a confirmed bachelor who never had a chance at an education, but together they enjoyed theater and photography. Although it took a while to accept this new man in her life, he eventually became a great-grandfather to my children, buying them presents when my grandmother was no longer able to do so.

Although I am still fortunate to have my husband Jim after more than 30 years of marriage, I do know what it is like to experience a tragic loss. Our daughter, Elizabeth, died at the age of 16 in 2006. After feeling lost and overwhelmed for several months, I, too, had to ask myself, "now what?"

Part of my new life path meant more time to devote to writing. I had a degree from Cornell University in Business Management and Marketing but had taken very few writing courses. So, I enrolled in a journalism class at Rockland Community College in Suffern, New York. While still a student, I was offered a job as a writer in the College's Campus Communications department. It was there I learned how to write press releases and interest the media in covering my news. This new-found skill helped me work on a cause dear to my heart—educating the public on how to prevent the kind of disabilities my daughter Elizabeth endured as a result of a common, yet little known virus, congenital cytomegalovirus (CMV). Most women of child-bearing age still haven't heard about it or how to prevent it, but I press on to change that.

Upon moving to Connecticut in 2010, I became a freelance writer. In 2014, I was offered a job as a columnist for the new magazine, *Pathfinder: A*

Companion Guide to the Widow/er's Journey. I became the author of the "Widow/ers of History" column because I like to write about dead people (they don't complain when their story is published). With their lives over, I could see how they did—or did not—move forward after the death of their spouse. The following widow/ers of history, with the exception of Abby Day Slocomb, are expanded versions of the articles that appeared in my column.

The following order of chapters is chronological, according to the date of death. Abby Day Slocomb, though, is featured last. She is a bit unique because her story isn't over yet. Unlike the others, she didn't rest from her earthly toils upon her death. Instead, she sent us a message—and a challenge—from beyond the grave. More on her later.

I chose many of these widowed people because their lives are intriguing. I wanted to understand what made them famous, what they did with their fame, and how they dealt with the loss of their spouse.

Some of these widowed are not internationally famous, but they had an impact on my life. Perhaps they will have an impact on yours.

Lisa Saunders, Mystic, Connecticut
May 24, 2016

1. KING HENRY VIII

Murderer as Widower

Author's note: Although King Henry VIII was responsible for launching England's first fighting fleet and creating the Church of England, he is most renowned for his ability to get out of a marriage in his time of "till death us depart."[1] Despite outliving four of his wives—two of whom he had beheaded – how many times did Henry actually consider himself a widower? A widower is defined as a man whose spouse has died and is not remarried. Is a man who has his wife executed considered a widower? How about a man who outlives a wife he decided wasn't a legitimate one in the first place?

Born June 28, 1491, in London, Henry Tudor was second in line to succeed his father, Henry VII, to the throne of England. His older brother, Arthur died after only three months of marriage at the age of 15, leaving a teenaged widow, who was Catherine of Aragon. Her parents were Ferdinand II and Queen Isabella I of Spain, who sponsored Christopher Columbus's first voyage to the New World.

Upon the death of Henry's father, Henry VII, in 1509, Henry wanted to marry his brother's widow, Catherine, immediately. So, on June 11, 1509, Henry, 17, married Catherine, 23.

1) *Catherine of Aragon*

The six-year age difference between Henry and Catherine made little difference to the happy newlyweds—Henry was in love. He put on pageants for Catherine, danced and wrote poems for her, and jousted in her honor. Catherine's firstborn was a stillborn daughter, but her second pregnancy resulted in their male heir—or so they thought. When Prince Henry was born New Year's Day 1511, city bells rang and wine flowed, but in less than two months, he was dead. While Catherine turned inward and sought comfort from God, Henry turned outward and sought other women. Catherine gave birth to another son, but he, too, died. After a stillborn son, she gave birth to a healthy child, Mary. Her sixth and final pregnancy resulted in a girl who died shortly thereafter.

Henry publicly acknowledged an illegitimate son he had with his mistress Bessie Blount by introducing him to court. On the day he did, not only was his wife in attendance, but so was someone else—Anne Boleyn. Henry was smitten by her and the thought of the sons she could give him—but she would not become his mistress.

Henry had to get rid of Catherine, but how? Surely their marriage must be cursed by God since she hadn't produced a son. Henry petitioned the pope to have it annulled pointing out that Catherine had been his sister-in-law, making it a marriage not allowed by the Church. Prior to their marriage, however, Henry had received a dispensation from the pope to marry Catherine. The pope would not give into Henry's demands for an annulment.

2) *Anne Boleyn*

Six years into Henry's struggle to get his marriage annulled, Anne Boleyn got pregnant. Henry broke away from Rome, formed the Church of England and declared his marriage to Catherine of Aragon invalid.

A friar had confronted Henry with a reference to a story from the Old Testament saying Henry was a king besotted with his own Jezebel – a woman who would bring him to ruin. The friar declared: "I say unto you as Elijah said to Ahab, 'The dogs shall lick your blood.'"[2] But Henry was not moved.

Henry secretly married Anne in January 1533. Henry's astrologers assured him the baby would be a boy. On September 7, 1533, Anne gave birth to Elizabeth I. Soon afterwards, Henry was pursuing the sweet and shy Jane Seymour, a lady in waiting.

Meanwhile, Catherine, who still declared her love for Henry and considered herself married to him in the sight of God, died in January 1536 while under guard in unhealthy conditions. She was given the funeral of a princess – not a queen.

Shortly after Catherine's death, Anne gave birth to a second stillborn baby – this time a boy. Enraged, Henry vowed his marriage to Anne cursed, would never sleep with her again, and decided to marry Jane Seymour. He had Anne detained at the Tower of London on several false charges including adultery and incest. Anne was found guilty and her marriage to Henry was annulled. On Friday, May 19, 1536, at 9 a.m., Anne's fur mantle was removed and her headdress put aside. She wore a plain linen cap with her hair carefully tucked up into it, baring her neck. A servant bandaged her eyes. With one swift motion, a French swordsman cut off Anne's head, which her attendants wrapped in a white cloth. They found an empty arrow box for her remains. It was too short for a full body, but Anne fit into it with her head placed at her side.

3) *Jane Seymour*

Henry and Jane were quietly married just days after Anne's execution. On October 12, 1537, Jane gave Henry what he so desperately wanted— his first legitimate male heir, Prince Edward. As Edward thrived, Jane drew weaker with a fever until she died less than two weeks after his birth.

Henry secluded himself to grieve and wore black. Jane was interred as Henry's queen at Windsor Castle in St. George's Chapel.

4) *Anne of Cleves*

More than two years after Jane's death, Henry believed he finally found a good political match for his next queen. The king's official painter was sent to Anne of Cleves, born in Germany, to paint her image. Henry liked the woman in the painting, but was repulsed by the sight and smell of her when she arrived just prior to their wedding. He went through with the marriage in January 1540, but just couldn't "perform" in bed. Fortunately for her, Henry found a way out of the marriage that didn't require the removal of her head. He learned of a pre-contract she had with another man that was considered binding, not merely a future promise to wed. Anne took the dissolution of their marriage well, especially since she received a sizable yearly income.

5) *Katherine Howard*

Six months after marrying Anne of Cleves, Henry was now free to marry his latest passion on July 28, 1540 – the 19-year-old Katherine Howard. Katherine was not only 30 years younger than Henry, but she also happened to be the first cousin of Anne Boleyn. Katherine renewed Henry's vigor and he lavished her with gifts and caresses—he was a king in love. But Katherine did not keep her mind on Henry for long before having affairs with men her own age. Henry was devastated at the news— then humiliated and angry. He publicly wept and vowed he would never marry again. After an investigation proved Katherine's adultery, she was sent to the Tower where she lost her head by axe on February 13, 1542. Her body was wrapped in a black cloak and she, like her cousin Anne Boleyn, was buried in the Tower chapel of St. Peter in Chains.

6) *Catherine Parr*

Despite Henry's depression over his love life and his declining health ever since a jousting accident left him with an injured leg, he was advised to find another wife to try for more male heirs in case Edward died young.

On July 12, 1543, Henry married the 31-year-old widow Catherine Parr. She was the daughter of a lady-in-waiting to Henry's first wife, Catherine of Aragon, and was named in honor of Catherine. After Henry made the standard pledge of "...to have and to hold from this day forward, for better for worse, in sickness and in health, till death us depart..." Catherine made similar vows with the additional promise of, "to be bonair and buxom in bed, till death us depart..."[3] Catherine Parr proved to be a very kind wife and was good to all of Henry's motherless children, Mary, Elizabeth and Edward. She only risked losing her head once on a charge of heresy, but Henry let the matter go when she sought his forgiveness. They seemed to enjoy each other, and when Henry was in pain and unable to move, Catherine stayed by his side and nursed his ulcerous leg.

On January 28, 1547, at the age of 55, Henry died. His will stated he wanted his remains placed alongside Jane Seymour's in St. George's Chapel in Windsor Castle. On the way to his final resting place, his lead coffin broke open allowing Henry's bodily fluids to seep onto the floor. A dog was seen licking up the bloody matter.[4]

Henry's son, Edward VI, inherited the throne but died shortly thereafter in 1553. The crown then fell to Henry's daughter Mary, daughter of his first wife, Catherine of Aragon, and upon Mary's death in 1558, to Henry's daughter, Elizabeth I, daughter of Anne Boleyn. Elizabeth's reign, known as the Elizabethan era, is also referred to as the "golden age" because great things were accomplished under her reign. Elizabeth never married and ruled England for almost 45 years until her death in 1603.

Questions for discussion

- Do you think that Henry VIII the widower deserves any sympathy or empathy?

- What emotional responses might one have if (s)he caused the death of their spouse?

2. MARTHA WASHINGTON

She left the bed

Author's note: As the loudest member of the Anna Warner Bailey Chapter of the Daughters of the American Revolution, I was asked to give a talk at a Martha Washington Tea fundraiser in a room without a microphone. Before my talk, I needed to learn something about Martha first. Wow! What a lady she was—so much more inspiring than indicated by those portraits of her wearing those floppy caps!

In December 1799, after 25 years of public service and just three years into retirement, George and Martha Washington were set to enjoy Christmas at Mount Vernon. But suddenly, George died – leaving Martha widowed for the second time.

In 1758, Martha had been a beautiful, wealthy widow of 27 with two surviving children when she met George, a handsome colonel, at a cotillion in Williamsburg, Virginia. At the time, George was fighting alongside the British in the French and Indian War. Powerfully attracted to each other after only a few meetings, George and Martha were already planning their future together. Just prior to their wedding on January 6, 1759, George resigned his military commission.

Martha brought her toddler Patsy, and Patsy's older brother Jacky, to Washington's Mount Vernon to begin the next chapter of their lives. George, age 26, wrote that he now had "an agreeable [sic] Consort for Life and hope to find more happiness in retirement than I ever experienced a wide and bustling World."[5]

George, whom Martha referred to as "Pappa," raised Martha's children as if they were his own. When Patsy was 12, she developed epilepsy. When she was 17, she died from a seizure in George's arms in 1773. George wrote that Patsy's death brought Martha to "the lowest ebb of [her] Misery."[6]

In 1775, George and Martha put aside their "happiness in retirement" when George took on the leadership of U.S. forces in the American Revolution. For eight years, Martha encamped every winter with George and his soldiers despite the freezing conditions and hard toil.

As the wife of the Commander-in-Chief, Martha carried heavy responsibilities. She listened to George's troubles, worked as his secretary, and represented him at official functions. She comforted sick and wounded soldiers, cooked and sewed for them, and sponsored social activities to boost camp morale.

Then came another blow—Martha lost her last surviving child, son Jacky, an enlisted soldier, at the age 26 from "camp fever." He left a family with four children under the age of five. Martha and George adopted the two youngest.

When the colonies finally achieved their independence, the couple thought they could retire to Mount Vernon. But once more, duty called when George was elected the country's first president. He was inaugurated in 1789.

As the first "First Lady," Martha now had the task of setting precedent for future first ladies in arranging major social events and parties. Looking to European customs as her guide, Martha held public receptions on Fridays and became renowned as a gracious hostess. Despite her popularity, however, she felt trapped by her position. She wrote, "I think I am more like a state prisoner than anything else, there are certain bounds set for me which I must not depart from..."[7]

Martha did, however, write, "I am still determined to be cheerful and happy, in whatever situation I may be; for I have also learned from experience that the greater part of our happiness or misery depends upon our dispositions, and not upon our circumstances."[8]

When her husband's second term as president ended in 1797, Martha thought they were finally released from duty. Although they felt obligated to entertain an endless stream of visitors, the couple assumed they were at Mount Vernon for good. Martha wrote to a friend, "The General and I feel like children just released from school or from a hard taskmaster, and we believe that nothing can tempt us to leave the sacred roof-tree again."[9]

With Christmas less than two weeks away on Thursday, December 12, 1799, George was outside in a mixture of snow, hail, and rain supervising the plantation. Instead of changing out of his wet riding clothes when he returned for dinner, he chose punctuality and dined as he was. The next morning, Friday, despite an emerging sore throat and snow on the ground, he went out to select trees for removal. Throughout the day, his voice became more hoarse and irritated.

At dawn on Saturday, December 14, George was having difficulty breathing. Doctors bled him and then dosed him with a mixture of molasses, butter, and vinegar to soothe his throat. But the liquid proved too difficult to swallow and almost caused him to suffocate. George knew he would not recover.

Late in the afternoon, he asked Martha to bring him his two wills from his study. He discarded one, and asked Martha to burn it. His surviving will stated that his slaves were to be freed and a new vault be built at Mount Vernon for the depositing of his remains along with those of other family members, as the old family vault was improperly situated and deteriorating. At 10 p.m., George requested to be "decently buried" and to "not let my body be put into the Vault in less than three days after I am dead."[10]

Before 11 p.m., at the age of 67, George passed away with Martha sitting at the foot of his bed.

Grief stricken, Martha closed up their bedroom and moved to a room in their third floor attic—one that she rarely left for the rest of her life. She felt so bereft that she couldn't attend George's funeral service on December 18. At age 68, Martha had now outlived her children and her two husbands.

As news of George's death reached the rest of the country, Martha received thousands of condolence letters and hundreds of requests for mementos, such as locks of George's hair. Exhausted and grieving—yet too numb to cry—she directed others to comply with all that was asked of her.

But one request proved too much to bear—one that even violated George's wishes. Congress wanted George's body removed from Mount Vernon for entombment in the country's new capital. In the end, with agony in her heart, Martha granted permission, leaving Congress to come up with the funds for construction of a mausoleum.

Martha took some comfort in her extended family, including her son Jacky's children, their spouses, and their children. She even welcomed visits from President John Adams and Abigail Adams and the other political figures, who came to pay their respects and visit George's body while it was still at Mount Vernon.

Martha wore mourning clothes, including a black shawl and a ring or locket containing a strand of George's hair. She often expressed her loneliness for George and her hope of joining him soon in death. To ensure some privacy, she burned all of their correspondence, missing only two letters trapped behind a drawer in her desk.

Sensing her own health was deteriorating, Martha laid out the white satin dress she wished to be buried in. She studied her Bible every day and looked forward to the day she would be reunited with George. On May 22, 1802, at age 71, Martha died of "severe fever." She did not breathe her last alone as her beloved granddaughter Nelly was nearby.

Martha was entombed with George, whose body was still in the family burial vault at Mount Vernon. It wasn't until nearly 30 years later in 1831 that George's body was finally moved to its permanent location. But it wasn't where Martha had feared. Instead of being taken for interment in Washington as planned, George and Martha's bodies were transferred together from the deteriorating family vault to a modest brick tomb built according to George's instructions decades earlier. Martha and George were finally at rest in the place they always longed to be—Mount Vernon.

Although there was a vaulted room built for George Washington two levels beneath the United States Capitol rotunda, it remains empty to this day. In 1832, when Congress asked George's great-nephew, John A. Washington, to allow the transfer of George's body to Washington, he refused. He would honor the intention expressed in his great-uncle's will.

Martha Washington finally got her way.

End note: Learn more about George and Martha Washington at Mount Vernon in Mount Vernon, Virginia. www.mountvernon.org, 703-780-2000.

Mount Vernon as it appears today. (Photograph by Jackie Tortora)

The brick tomb completed in 1831 per instructions in George Washington's will as it appears today. Behind the iron gate are two marble sarcophagi, one inscribed "Washington," the other, "Martha, Consort of Washington." (Photograph by Paul J. Tortora Jr.)

The empty vaulted room built to hold George Washington's remains as it appears today. It is located two levels beneath the United States Capitol rotunda. (Photograph by Paul J. Tortora Jr.)

Questions for discussion

- How do you judge Martha's decision to live in the 3rd floor bedroom after George's death?

- What do you think of the tradition of wearing black?

- Where do you think George should have been buried?

3. MARY TODD LINCOLN

Complicated grief

Author's note: After spending years researching my great-great grandparents' Civil War love letters for my book, Ever True: A Union Private and His Wife, *I felt a personal connection to President Lincoln. When Private Charles McDowell of the New York 9th Heavy Artillery first met Lincoln in Washington, D.C., he wrote to his teenaged wife, Nancy: "We have [Secretary of State] Seward down here about every other day, and sometimes he fetches Old Abe with him and [he] looks about like any old farmer." A surgeon from Charles's regiment attended the play at Ford's Theatre the night Lincoln was assassinated, so I included his account of that night in the following story. Of the assassination, Charles wrote to Nancy, "The army felt very bad when they heard of Lincoln's death. I hope they will catch the band that done it."*

It was April 14, 1865—Good Friday—and the nation's capital was rejoicing. General Robert E. Lee had surrendered his Confederate Army days earlier on April 9. With the war virtually over, Mary and President Abraham Lincoln finally had a chance for happiness. The long, heavy burden of the conflict was very personal because Mary's family sided with the south. Mary adamantly supported her husband, however, and the Union cause.

Throughout this turbulent time, the couple also endured the death of their 11-year-old son Willie in 1862. Dying of typhoid fever in the disease-ridden capital, Willie was their second son to pass away. They now had their 12-year-old son, Tad, and their firstborn, 21-year-old Capt. Robert Todd Lincoln. Robert had arrived from Appomattox Court House, Virginia, in time to have breakfast with his father.

President Lincoln was now 56, nine years older than Mary. They were an unlikely couple as she had come from money and a formal education, while Abraham Lincoln came from poverty and was self-educated, but they shared a passion for politics and literature. Despite her family's disapproval about his background, Mary married Abraham, a politician and lawyer, in 1842 in Springfield, Illinois.

Mary and Abraham loved attending the theater and opera. Theater gave President Lincoln some relief from his relentless worries over the war. The couple decided to celebrate the war's end by attending the comedy "My American Cousin" at Ford's Theatre.

Mary reminisced in a letter about the open carriage ride she took with Abraham to relax before the show: "I never saw him so supremely cheerful—his manner was even playful...I said to him, laughingly, 'Dear Husband, you almost startle me by your great cheerfulness,' he replied, 'and well I may feel so, Mary, I consider this day, the war, has come to a close—and then added, 'We must both be more cheerful in the future – between the war & the loss of our darling Willie – we have both been very miserable."[11] They discussed future plans to travel west to California and then perhaps to Europe. Abraham also wanted to make a special pilgrimage to Jerusalem, a city he yearned to see.

The Lincolns invited Clara Harris, the daughter of a New York senator, and her fiancé to join them at the theater. Arriving late to the theater, President Lincoln acknowledged the prolonged cheers from the audience with a slight bow and sat in the upholstered rocking chair beside Mary in an upper private box. Their guests were to their right.

The interior of the President's Box at Ford's Theatre is pictured here in 1980. (Photograph by Carol M. Highsmith; courtesy of Ford's Theatre)

Mary snuggled close to Abraham. Clinging to his arm, she whispered, "What will Miss Harris think of my hanging on to you so?"

Lincoln replied, "She won't think anything about it."[12]

In the third act, when one of the actors delivered his punch line, "Well, I guess I know enough to turn you inside out, you sockdologizing old man-trap,"[13] the crowd burst into laughter – and a shot was fired by John Wilkes Booth into President Lincoln's head. Abraham's arm jerked up convulsively. For a moment, Mary and Clara were frozen in their seats. Then Mary, covered in Abraham's blood, held Abraham in the rocker so he wouldn't fall to floor. She began screaming and sobbing wildly.

Surgeon Dr. Samuel A. Sabin of the New York 9th Heavy Artillery was in the audience. He wrote to his wife: "I ran immediately to the president's box…As soon as I saw the wound I saw there was no hope. Some brandy was brought and given, he could not swallow. The bullet entered the head behind the left ear and penetrated the brain…"

President Lincoln was carried to a private residence across the street. Sabin added: "Mrs. Lincoln was nearly crazy, and as she followed from the theater she cried in frantic words, 'O, my poor husband; oh, my poor husband!' The president, of course, was entirely unconscious…"[14]

President Lincoln, too tall for the bed in the shabby back rental room, was placed diagonally across it. A gas lamp was lit, emitting an eerie green light. When Mary entered the room, she fell to her knees beside the bed. Weeping and using intimate names, she pleaded with him to speak to her. But all Abraham could do was breath in and out. When their son Robert arrived, he took Mary to the front parlor and tried to get her to rest. She alternated between wailing and quiet disbelief. She returned to Abraham's bedside every hour or so. Seeing his engorged and swollen eye turning purple, she cried out, "Oh that my little Taddie might see his father before he died!"[15] When Abraham's face started to twitch, she collapsed on the floor and screamed in horror.

Someone yelled, "Take that woman out and do not let her in again!"[16]

As dawn broke, a heavy rain beat against the windows. Mary entered the bedroom to see her husband for the last time. She pressed her lips to his face and said, "Love, live but one moment to speak to me once – to speak to our children."[17]

At 7:22 a.m., the doctor told Mary, "It is over. The President is no more."[18] He laid silver half-dollars on President Lincoln's eyelids—an ancient Greek custom to pay the ferryman who transported souls across the river from the world of the living to the world of the dead. The surgeon general slipped a sheet over Abraham's face, and the pastor mouthed a prayer.

Mary was now a widow at the age of 47 after 23 years of marriage. No longer able to stand up, she was taken to the White House to be cared for. Refusing to enter the family's bedrooms, she finally agreed to use a tiny spare bedroom. Her seamstress and closest confidant, former slave Elizabeth Keckly, was called in to comfort her.

When Keckly arrived, Abraham's body was lying in a guest room where three years earlier he had wept over their son Willie's coffin. Robert, now the head of the household, tried to comfort his mother. Tad crouched at the foot of Mary's bed. He couldn't bear his mother's shrieking and begged her to stop.

Mary remained inconsolable and did not attend Abraham's funeral in the East Room. She relived Abraham's final hours over and over, often hysterical and at times, delirious. Her emotional needs drained all around her, but Keckly remained at her side and slept in her room. Some thought the tragedy had caused her to lose her mind. Mary was so overwhelmed and heartbroken, it took her six weeks to pack her numerous crates and trunks and vacate the White House.

Mary found it hard to give up her life as Mrs. President. Filled with guilt by her ambition to see Abraham become president, she said, "My poor husband! Had he never been president, he might be living today. Alas! All is over with me!"[19]

Mary couldn't bear to return to their home in Springfield, Illinois, without Abraham and their son Willie. She thought she would lose all ability to reason if she did. She chose to move to Chicago with her sons, saying that was where Lincoln had wanted to retire. Tad went to school, Robert went to work at a law firm and Mary kept to herself, wanting little to do with the outside world.

Sympathy notes poured in from all over. Queen Victoria's note included the words, "No-one can better appreciate than I can who am myself utterly broken hearted by the loss of my own beloved Husband, who was the light of my Life—my stay—my all, –what your sufferings must be; and I earnestly pray that you may be supported by Him to whom Alone the sorely stricken can look for comfort in this hour of heavy affliction."[20]

Unlike Queen Victoria and Abraham, Mary did not look to the faith that so sustained them, but rather sought comfort in spiritualism, as she had after Willie died.

On July 11, 1865, Mary wrote to Elizabeth Blair Lee, one of the first women to come to the White House to comfort her, saying, "Never, in my life, have I had the least idea, of the meaning of the word, Desolation!…I am realizing, day by day, hour by hour, how insupportable life is, without, the presence of the One, who loved me & my sons so dearly & in return, was idolized. Tell me, how can I live, without my Husband, any longer? This is my first awakening thought, each morning & as I watch the waves of the turbulent lake, under our windows, I sometimes feel I should like to go, under them."[21]

A month later Mary wrote to her, "Time does not soften it, nor can I ever be reconciled to my loss, until the grave closes over the remembrance, and I am again reunited with him."[22]

Abraham died without a will, so Mary had to wait for his estate to be settled—and of that, she would only get a third, having to share the rest with her sons. Mary confided in Keckly that she owed $27,000 as a result of her extravagant spending on jewelry and other luxuries.

Unlike other women of her time, Mary didn't want to rely on a male relative to support her. Mary had an irrational fear of poverty and it overwhelmed her. Worried that her creditors would call in her debts now that President Lincoln was dead, and as of yet unable to convince Congress to give her a pension, Mary asked Keckly to help her find a broker in New York to sell her elaborate dresses. She figured people would want something that had belonged to President Lincoln's wife—but very few did. Instead, Mary was ridiculed in the press for trying to sell old clothes.

Mary continued to tell everyone of her dire financial condition much to the embarrassment of her son, Robert. Mary also continued to spend money with abandon on things she didn't need.

In addition to her money worries, Mary was mortified by a biographical account of Abraham's life that claimed he hadn't loved her, having never gotten over the death of Ann Rutledge, his fiancée before her. When Keckly herself wrote a book about Mary, which included Mary's letters to her (Keckly didn't know the publisher was going to publish them), Mary felt utterly betrayed. She took Tad to Europe to live abroad for a while to escape the humiliation following the book's publication in 1868.

In 1870, Congress finally granted Mary an annual pension of $3,000. In May 1871, Mary and Tad, 18, returned to Chicago from Europe. Robert was now a married Chicago attorney. Two months later, Tad died of pleurisy. This death was too much for Mary's already fragile mental health. She experienced periods of mild insanity such as thinking gas was invented by the devil and would only use candles in her room. She had several strange symptoms, which many believed confirmed her insanity. In retrospect, it is now believed some of her symptoms, such as the feeling of needles running through her body, indicated she suffered from diabetes.

Mary spent the rest of her life visiting doctors and spiritualists in search of relief from her mental and physical suffering, which included the inability to sleep. In May of 1875, Robert had his mother declared insane and committed to a mental asylum. During the public trial, Robert cited her erratic behavior, bizarre spiritualism that included hearing voices, and her uncontrolled spending. He felt she needed constant care and he needed to control her finances.

Again, Mary felt betrayed—and by her only surviving son. The day after being declared insane by the jury, Mary tried to kill herself by overdosing on laudanum (a drug that includes opium), but was prevented by a hotel druggist who recognized her and gave her something harmless instead.

Four months later, Mary secured her release from the asylum with the help of her sister. In June 1876, the court declared Mary "restored to reason."[23] Unable to face people who would regard her as a lunatic, Mary spent the next four years abroad, seeing the things she and Abraham had dreamed about on their last day together. Unfortunately, she was too ill and depressed to enjoy them. Despite her love of theater, she was never known to enter one again after that terrible night at Ford's Theatre.

Mary eventually returned to Springfield, Illinois, to her sister's home, where she spent the rest of her life in her room with the shades drawn, lit only by candles. She died on July 15, 1882, at the age of 64. Her death certificate listed cause of death as paralysis, but some believe her symptoms suggested diabetic coma.

Mary's coffin was placed in the parlor where she and Abraham had married nearly 40 years earlier. Entombed with Abraham at Oak Ridge Cemetery in Springfield, Mary finally got what she so longed for since April 15, 1865—to be reunited with her husband.

Author's note: When my great-great grandmother, Nancy McDowell, died in 1931, her New York obituary stated: "MRS. MCDOWELL IS DEAD - SHOOK HANDS WITH LINCOLN. With the death of Mrs. Nancy McDowell, the town of Sodus loses the distinction of having a resident who could boast of having shaken hands and talked with the martyred Lincoln..." Nancy likely met Lincoln when she lived with Charles for nearly a year in Washington, D.C., where she baked apple pies for soldiers.

For more information about Abraham Lincoln's assassination, visit Ford's Theatre in Washington, D.C.
www.fords.org, (202) 347-4833.

Questions for discussion

- What do you think explains Mary's difficulties in adjusting to life as a widow?

- Do you think Mary's son was justified in his behavior toward his mother?

- Do you feel that Mary's interest in spiritualism influenced her recovery?

4. MARK TWAIN

Adopted granddaughters

Publisher's note: We all know that Mark Twain was an absolute genius. I think his brilliance showed through when he "adopted" granddaughters to help him move forward after his devastating losses. Our author has been known to borrow other people's children since the death of her daughter. One of the big problems, you see, is that the survivor still has so much love to give; they need a place to pour it.

Widowhood was hard on humorist Samuel Clemens, better known by his penname, Mark Twain. When Olivia ("Livy") died at age 58, Samuel, at 68, had also outlived two of their four children. He had no grandchildren. Samuel said, "I am tired & old; I wish I were with Livy."[24]

He describes that time of his life as "washing about in a forlorn sea of banquets & speechmaking."[25] He began wearing white suits believing that light colored clothes "enlivens the spirit."[26]

The famous American writer knew grief and hardship at an early age. Born the sixth of seven children on November 30, 1835, the Hannibal, Missouri, resident left school after fifth grade to earn a living after his father died. He worked as a printer's apprentice and later wrote articles for newspapers. Other careers included riverboat pilot on the Mississippi River, a volunteer in the Confederate Army, silver prospector, and travel writer. While on a steamship tour of Europe and the Holy Land, he met Charles Langdon who showed him a picture of his sister Olivia. Sam thought she was just beautiful and when he later visited their home in Elmira, New York, he proposed to Olivia a few days later. She said no, but he was welcome to write letters.

So Sam did what he did best—write. He wrote about the mundane, such as his trip to Mystic, Connecticut, in November 1869: "I had to submit to the customary & exasperating drive around town in a freezing open buggy this morning to see the wonders of the village. They always consist of the mayor's house; the ex-mayor's house…the public school with its infernal architecture…& I must sit and shiver & stare at a melancholy grove of skeleton trees & listen while my friend gushes enthusiastic statistics & dimensions…"[27]

He also wrote: "Livy, you are so interwoven with the very fibres of my being that if I were to lose you it seems to me that to lose memory & reason at the same time would be a blessing to me."[28]

After two years of courting, 24-year-old Olivia married 34-year-old Samuel in her family's living room on February 2, 1870. Sam couldn't believe his good fortune--he got to sleep in the same bed with the "only sweetheart I have ever loved."[29]

The couple moved to Buffalo, New York, where their son, Langdon, was born. In 1871, Sam moved his family to Hartford, Connecticut, the most prosperous city in the country. In 1872, Olivia gave birth to their second child Susy, but nine weeks later, their happiness was shattered when Langdon died at the age of two from diphtheria. Two more daughters followed: Clara in 1874 and Jean in 1880. From 1874-1891, they lived in their exquisitely designed home on Farmington Avenue.

The Mark Twain House & Museum on Farmington Ave, Hartford, Connecticut, pictured in 2012. (Photograph by John Groo Photography; courtesy of Mark Twain House & Museum)

Sam's life on Farmington Avenue were his happy years of encouraging his daughters to present plays and creating new stories for them every night by incorporating every item on their mantel piece. He also wrote some of his best-loved novels during that time: *The Adventures of Tom Sawyer* (1876), *Adventures of Huckleberry Finn* (1884), and *A Connecticut Yankee in King Arthur's Court* (1889).

Sam's downfall was his lavish spending style and a series of bad investments, which put him into bankruptcy. Determined to pay off everyone he owed, he went on a worldwide lecture tour, taking Olivia and daughter Clara with him. Daughters Jean and Susy, who was herself a writer and considered Sam's favorite, stayed behind in the U.S. with friends. In 1896, tragedy struck the family again when they learned Susy died from meningitis while visiting their Hartford home. They would never again live in that house—Olivia couldn't bear the thought of it.

In 1903, Olivia became ill with asthma and suffered a heart condition. Doctors felt Samuel would exhaust her so limited his time with her to two minutes a day. Sam wrote notes to her, pushing them under the door: "Good morning, dear heart, & thank you for your dear greeting. I think of you all the time…"[30]

When Sam took Olivia to Italy in October 1903 to winter there, the Italian doctors also enforced a two-minute bedside rule. Sometimes Sam snuck in anyway. Their servant, Katy Leary, recalled: "She'd put her arms around his neck the first thing and he'd hold her soft, and give her one of them tender kisses…It was a love that was more than earthly love—it was heavenly."[31]

On the Sunday evening of June 5, 1904, when Sam went in to say goodnight, Olivia was gone. That evening Sam wrote, "She has been dead two hours…She was my life, and she is gone; she was my riches, and I am a pauper."[32]

So began Sam's season of "washing about in a forlorn sea…" While living in Redding, Connecticut, the answer to Samuel's loneliness finally came to him when the mother of a 14-year old girl insisted on meeting him when they traveled to America. The teenage girl reminded him of his joy in raising his own daughters when they were young. Sam later referred to that meeting as a "fortunate day, a golden day, and my heart has never been empty of grandchildren since."[33]

While on a trip to Bermuda, Samuel met several more girls. It occurred to him to "adopt" them and form a literary and arts club "with wholesome rules for membership."[34] He called these girls the "Bermudian angelfish" and their club, the "Aquarium." More than 300 letters were exchanged, with the correspondence becoming Sam's "chief occupation and delight."[35] He invited the girls (with their mothers), ranging in ages from 10-14, to visit his home.

In one letter to teenager Dorothy Sturgis on August 3, 1908, Sam included a recent photograph. He wrote "… The cat is Tammany, the pride of the place. You will notice that I have become extraordinarily hump-shouldered. The doctors say it will never diminish, but will increase. They say it is due to bad circulation, lack of exercise, & excessive smoking. I do not care. It is good enough shape, & I like it."[36]

After Dorothy visited in September of 1908, Clemens encouraged her to compose a sign to burglars as his house had been robbed recently. The sign read, "…If you want the basket, put the kittens in the brass thing. Do not make a noise — it disturbs the family. … Please close the door when you go away."[37]

In 1909, Sam's health declined and his letters to the girls dwindled. He didn't like that they were growing up. In addition, when his daughter Clara learned of the club upon her return from Europe in September 1908, "she sensed scandal in the offing and made her father sharply curtail his activities."[38]

According to the article, "Mark Twain's 'Aquarium'," by Dennis Gaffney (2008): "Clemens' last reference to one of the angelfish was made on a ship returning from a visit to Bermuda in 1910, in which he wrote that one girl, Helen Allen, should protect the 'diamond' of her innocence and be 'cautious, watchful, wary.'"

Sam finally found satisfying companionship when his daughter Jean, who had been living in an epilepsy colony as a result of her seizures, moved back home. But even that delight was grabbed from him when she was found dead Christmas Eve morning in the bathroom, having died during a seizure. She had been so happy the night before preparing their home for Christmas and buying presents. On December 24, 1909, at 11 a.m., Sam wrote, "I lost Susy thirteen years ago; I lost her mother—her incomparable mother!—five and half years ago; Clara has gone away to live in Europe; and now I have lost Jean. How poor I am, who was once so rich! ...and I sit here—writing, busying myself, to keep my heart from breaking."[39] Sam also felt pity for Jean's dog, though in general he was not fond of dogs, "because they bark when there is no occasion for it; but I have liked this one from the beginning, because he belonged to Jean and because he never barks except when there is occasion—which is not oftener than twice a week."[40]

Two days after Jean's death, on December 26, he wrote: "The dog came to see me at eight o'clock this morning. He was very affectionate, poor orphan! My room will be his quarters hereafter."[41]

Sam had spent his last years in his bed and now, even more so. His bed had become his true home. He and Livy had purchased it in Venice for their Hartford home. They would prop their pillows up at the foot of the bed so they could admire the carved cherubs at the head.

Sam was weary of living and waited for his time to come. Four months after Jean's death, Sam died on April 21, 1910, at the age of 74. Beside him on his bed lay his glasses and the book, *French Revolution* by Thomas Carlyle. He finally had his wish to join Livy, along with their three children who predeceased him, at Woodlawn Cemetery in Elmira, New York. He missed the birth of his biological granddaughter, Nina Clemens Gabrilowitsch, on August 19, 1910.

End note: To learn more about Samuel Clemens, visit the Mark Twain Boyhood Home & Museum in Hannibal, Missouri, marktwainmuseum.org, and the Mark Twain House & Museum in Hartford, Connecticut, marktwainhouse.org.

The Clemens family's burial plot is pictured in summer of 2012 at the Woodlawn Cemetery in Elmira, New York. (Photograph by Sean McKim)

Questions for Discussion

- What activities helped Mark Twain raise his very low spirits after the death of his wife, Olivia?

- He was told by his doctors to exercise more and quit smoking, but he did not care. How do you feel about his lack of concern for his health?

---

5. HETTY GREEN

Miserly Enigma

Publisher's note: A wealthy widow – not exactly an oxymoron, but certainly very unusual for a woman of the 1800s. She caught the attention of her contemporaries, who read about her in the newspapers, and then the world when she made it into the Guinness Book of World Records. *I'm thrilled that Lisa chose this enigma of a woman to investigate. I couldn't wait to find out if those odd tales about her were really true!*

Listed in the *Guinness Book of World Records* as the "Greatest Miser," Hetty Green wasn't just famous for pinching pennies—she was famous for making them grow. She was heralded as the richest woman in the world and one of the first to make a fortune on Wall Street. Her success, eccentricities, and possibly her ever-worn, old black dress, led to the nickname "Witch of Wall Street."

According to the *Guinness Book of Worlds Records*, Hetty "was so mean that her son had to have his leg amputated because of the delays in finding a free medical clinic…She herself lived off cold oatmeal because she was too mean to heat it…"[42]

Hetty's fortune did not begin with an inheritance from her husband who predeceased her, but rather from her father. He became rich in the whaling industry during the days when oil from hunted whales lit homes and lighthouses, and lubricated the machinery of the world.

Hetty was born Henrietta Howland Robinson on November 21, 1834, into a Quaker family in New Bedford, Massachusetts, the whaling capital of New England at the height of the whaling industry. She was the only surviving child of Edward Robinson and Abby Howland (the daughter of wealthy Isaac Howland Jr.).

From the time she was a young girl, it was Hetty's job to read the financial pages to her grandfather because of his failing eyesight, and at the age of 15, she became her father's bookkeeper. She grew fascinated in trade news from New York and her father regularly gave her lessons in finance. Hetty said, "My father taught me never to owe anyone anything. Not even kindness."[43]

Hetty accompanied her father on errands, such as collecting on loans, and visited the waterfront where her father would shout at dock workers to quickly unload as many as 3,000 barrels or more of oil from an incoming ship.* This oil was then converted into lamp oil, candles and watch oil. (Herman Melville, author of *Moby Dick*, briefly visited New Bedford before shipping out on a whaling voyage in January 1841. It is possible he saw Hetty as a little girl with her father).

Even as a young woman, Hetty hated spending money to dress in the latest styles. But even by Quaker standards, Hetty was unfashionable and preferred to dress in castoffs. She also cursed like a dockworker. According to the article, "The Strange Case of Hetty Green," in the *New York Times*, "Shamed friends in after years would give [Hetty] good clothing to wear at parties, but she would keep the new clothes magpie-fashion and show up at the party as sloppy-looking as ever. As a girl, in New Bedford, her aunt used to chide her for demeaning the family name by 'running about town clad as wretchedly as if she was one of the orphans of some sailor lost at sea.'"[44]

It was hoped that attending a fashionable school in Massachusetts and spending time with relatives in New York would soften Hetty around the edges. But when her father sent her $1,200 to purchase gowns for the social season, Hetty spent only $200 and put the rest in the bank. She boasted that at her "coming out" party she was able to save money by extinguishing the candles while the guests were still leaving.

When, by society's standards, Hetty was entering her spinster years at the age of 30 in 1865, her father introduced her to a business associate of his, the 44-year-old bachelor, Edward Henry Green. A prominent business man from Bellows Falls, Vermont, Edward had already earned a fortune trading tea, silk and other products. He didn't need Hetty's inheritance. Hetty's father, whose opinion she valued more than any other, liked and respected Edward.

Perhaps it was Hetty's interest in business combined with her clever wit and pretty, big blue eyes that attracted Edward. Edward, an Episcopalian, was gentle, fun-loving and enjoyed spending money on fine clothes, food and wine. He was also a generous tipper. Hetty didn't mind his love of the finer thing as long as he didn't spend her money to get them.

According to Edward's friend, Hetty agreed to marry Edward when, instead of sending her the Valentine's Day card he purchased for her, he accidentally mailed her an envelope containing a receipt for a tailor's bill. The bill was for a very cheap suit of clothes. Hetty admired Edward's sense of economy over this suit, and they became engaged.

Hetty, 33, and Edward, 46, married in New York in 1867, and sailed to London to live. There, Hetty gave birth to two children – Ned and Sylvia. Edward enjoyed the comfortable life his money could buy and paid all the bills, freeing Hetty up to invest and reinvest her $5 million inheritance. The strategies she learned from her father paid off and her money quickly multiplied. She bought low, sold high, and never panicked when other investors did.

In the spring of 1874, Edward brought Hetty and the children back to his hometown of Bellows Falls, Vermont. He bought a large home with a widow's walk on a bluff overlooking the Connecticut River. He called it the Tucker House after his grandfather who was a previous owner. When Edward's neighbors met Hetty for the first time, they were shocked by her shabby wardrobe, unkempt hair and sailor's language. They felt sorry for Edward who was embarrassed by Hetty's haggling with neighborhood shopkeepers over every bill.

Edward was no match for Hetty when she determined to do away with luxuries such as his prized two-horse barouche that he enjoyed riding in with his family. Hetty decided they didn't need such an extravagance so she sold the fine carriage and horses and paid $10 for an old horse and small jump seat wagon that barely fit them all.

A blow to the family came when Ned's leg required amputation at 14 as a result of a sledding accident several years earlier. It was rumored that it could have been saved if Hetty had sought proper medical care sooner. It is true, Hetty dressed in tattered clothes to receive free medical help in a clinic, but she had sought other medical help as well.

The final blow to Hetty and Edward's marriage came when Edward's ill-advised business speculations failed dramatically, plunging him over $700,000 in debt to the financial house where Hetty had investments. Refusing to pay her husband's debts, Hetty withdrew what securities she could from the bankrupt firm and deposited them in Chemical National Bank. Hetty never officially divorced Edward, but she took the children and moved to New York. Edward was broke with no money to rebuild his fortune.

In New York, Hetty could finally live the way she saw fit—not in a mansion hobnobbing with the millionaires on 5th Avenue, but in cheap rented apartments and rooming houses among storekeepers and washerwomen. She rented by the month to avoid showing an established residency and paying personal property tax. Not wanting to pay for office space, she managed her investments daily at any available desk at Chemical National Bank. To avoid restaurant bills, she'd arrive with a metal pail containing dry oatmeal, which she later mixed with water to heat on the radiator for lunch.

Hetty and Edward were known to share holiday meals together. As they aged, they eventually became friends again and saw each other regularly. As Edward became increasingly infirm, it was Hetty who nursed him. At times, Edward lived in an apartment above hers in Hoboken, New Jersey, so she could visit and read to him in the evenings.

Hetty and Edward lived together in the summer of 1900 in the Tucker House, that now belonged to Hetty. Extremely sick, Edward lingered for two years lying in his bed and looking out the window. In October of 1901, doctors gave him only a short time to live so Hetty stayed to tend to Edward while managing her investments from another room. Although she still traveled back and forth to New York when necessary, she did what she could to keep Edward comfortable, getting up three times a night to make sure the nurses were awake and attentive.

Edward died peacefully on March 19, 1902, at the age of 81. He was buried in the nearby Episcopal cemetery where he joined several generations of Greens. Of all the funeral flowers received, the most striking – a large arrangement of Laurel and Easter lilies – were from Hetty.

As a widow, Hetty continued to make headlines—especially when she bought a pistol. Fearing she would be robbed and killed for her money, she wanted everyone to know she had a gun.

When Hetty suffered a slight attack of indigestion, she became afraid of her own death. Although she still had no desire to establish residency anywhere, there was one place she wanted to call home—her final home. She wanted to spend eternity next to Edward. To ensure this, she had to become an Episcopalian to be buried in his cemetery. Hetty was baptized into the Episcopalian Church in July of 1912.

Four years later, Hetty died at the home of her son after several paralytic strokes on July 3, 1916. She was 82. The headline in the *New York Times* read: "Hetty Green Dies, Worth $100,000,000…Invested Heavily in Bonds and Mortgages in Recent Years—Stock Market Not Affected." They not only featured her business dealings, which included lending vast sums during the panic of 1907 to "hard pressed individuals and firms," her son was heavily quoted on how misunderstood his mother was. "When it becomes known that a person has money to lend you have no idea of the requests that come for it...begging letters and letters from unbalanced people...mother never told of her charities, though they were many. The sums of $500, $1,000 and $10,000 she gave away were many …" For example, Hetty continued to pay her old, longtime bookkeeper his wage even though he slept all day at his desk.

Hetty's neighbors in her cheap lodging establishments testified of many instances when she insisted on paying them for a kindness done to her. According to the *New York Times* (July 9, 1916), "Probably many a discouraged fellow out of work never attributed his newly found job to the shabby old lady on the floor above, while many a poor woman, at wit's end to know where the month's rent was coming from, never ascribed the envelope containing the necessary amount, which was slipped under her door, to the queer old woman across the hall."

The articles ended with a conversation she had with a visiting friend shortly before her death. Her friend said to Hetty, "You have been a very patient invalid so kind and good to every one about you."

Hetty replied, "God has been good and kind to me, why shouldn't I be good and kind to others?"[45]

Hetty left all but $25,000 of her fortune to her two children. At her funeral in Vermont, where she lay in a plain, wooden coffin, the Episcopal church choir sang the 19th century song, "There is a blessed home." Her body finally found a blessed home when it was taken to the shady spot where Edward was buried. With no money to fight over, spend, save or invest, Edward and Hetty are finally enjoying their eternal rest together. Their shared modest obelisk bears Edward's name and beneath his:

HETTY H.R. GREEN
HIS WIFE

* End note: From 1849 to 1859, Hetty's father, Edward (Black Hawk) Robinson, was the principal owner of the *Charles W. Morgan*, now the only wooden whale ship left in the world. Hetty's son, Col. Edward H.R. Green, later owned it and put it on public display. After Col. Green's death, ownership of the *Charles W. Morgan* was transferred to Mystic Seaport in Mystic, Connecticut, where she is a permanent exhibit that people can board and explore.

The *Charles W. Morgan* is pictured here undergoing restoration in 2011 at Mystic Seaport.

Questions for Discussion

- Hetty achieved her financial goals. Do you think her wealth contributed to her happiness later in life?

- How do you think money influenced her relationship with her husband?

6. FRANCES SAWYER WOLFE

The web families weave

Author's note: Upon moving to the seafaring village of Mystic, Connecticut, from Suffern, New York, in 2010, I was intrigued by all the homes featuring widow's walks and graveyards with "Lost at Sea" markers. In the Elm Grove Cemetery along the Mystic River, I marveled at the beauty of the "garden cemetery" designed in the shape of an elm tree—a configuration easily discernible in satellite images. More than 13,000 souls, many on Mystic's "Who's Who" list of 19th century

31

ship builders and sea captains, are buried or remembered there with a marker. I pondered the tall obelisk depicting the steamship, City of Waco, *and its statement about how Captain Thomas E. Wolfe died piloting her when it caught fire off the port of Galveston in 1875. He was 44 when his ship erupted into flames and sank. His body was found two miles away. He literally died with his boots on—a dramatic end to a man who led a dramatic life. I felt sorry for his widow, Frances Jane Sawyer, buried nearby as she outlived him by more than 40 years. How lonely she must have been all those years. Or so I thought...*

How could Frances Jane Wolfe, the mother of three teenagers, bear hearing the details of her husband's death in Texas's deadliest maritime disaster on November 9, 1875? Imagining her husband's struggle to survive after his steamer erupted into flames that stormy night must have plagued her incessantly. Some believed the volatile cargo of lamp oil may have led to the loss of all 56 passengers and crew. Only three bodies were recovered—one of them her husband's. Captain Wolfe's body appeared to have burn marks on it and looked as though he had been trying to cut his boots off.

The Wolfes were from Mystic, Connecticut, a ship building community near the Long Island Sound. Born January 20, 1831, Captain Thomas E. Wolfe's life of adventure began at age 14 when he went out to sea as a ship's boy. A year later, he embarked on a whaling voyage to the Indian Ocean for nearly two years. During the California Gold Rush, Wolfe caught gold fever with two Mystic friends, Charles Sisson and Ransford Ashby, and together they sailed around Cape Horn to California in 1850.

Unsuccessful in their search for gold, and probably realizing more died of scurvy than found gold, the three young men headed back to Mystic. In August of 1852, Captain Wolfe, at age 21, married Frances J. Sawyer, age 19. A year earlier, Frances's older sister, Ann Sawyer, married Wolfe's gold rush companion, Charles Sisson, who was also a sea captain.

Frances and Thomas Wolfe had three children who survived infancy—two sons and a daughter. It is unlikely Frances ever became accustomed to her husband's dangerous occupation. During the Civil War, Captain Wolfe transported supplies from New York to New Orleans. When his ship, *Texana,* was captured by Confederates and burned in 1863, he was taken prisoner. Initially, Thomas's letters to Frances from Castle Thunder Prison in Richmond, Virginia, were upbeat because he assumed he would be included in a prisoner exchange. He encouraged her not to worry and to keep their three children comfortable. But as time slipped by, Thomas revealed his growing despair in his letter dated December 23, 1863:

Dear Wife,

...The children must have grown very much since I left home it is most nine months. It makes me homesick to look out of my prison window and see little children the age of ourn a playing in the street.

... the hours hang heavy. My former occupation of a sailor may have fitted me somewhat to bare the disappointments and hardships of prison life. it is worse than working to the westward off Cape Horn for one will occasionally gain a little on their course their but here it is the same thing every day...

In the following month he wrote: *"If I was home I think I should enjoy the skating...but I see no prospect of getting there very soon...I expect little Emma has forgot her da da."*[46]

Later transferred to North Carolina's Salisbury Prison, Wolfe and his fellow prisoners were cold and starving. On the rainy night of December 18, 1864, he made a daring escape with four companions and headed north. During their grueling, 340-mile trek through enemy territory that included the Blue Ridge Mountains, he faced sleepless nights on the frozen ground, hours hidden under damp fodder, barking dogs, and a companion's snoring that put them at constant risk of discovery. Although Wolfe could barely limp along as a result of his sprained ankle, he provided some comic relief with stories of his past adventures.

One of the escapees, *New York Daily Tribune* journalist Albert D. Richardson, wrote in his memoir, *The Secret Service, the Field, the Dungeon, and the Escape* (1865), about a 12-mile section of road that crossed a frigid stream 29 times with only foot logs for pedestrians. "Cold and stiff, we discovered that crossing the smooth, icy logs in the darkness was a hazardous feat. Wolfe was particularly lame, and slipped several times into the icy torrent, but managed to flounder out without much delay."[47]

It was the food, warmth and guidance offered by slaves and Union sympathizers with secret handshakes, plus Wolfe's knowledge of celestial navigation, that brought them to safety. Richardson recalled, "We walked about a mile through the dense woods, when Captain Wolfe, who had been all the time declaring that the North Star was on the wrong side of us, convinced our pilot [guide] that he had mistaken the road, and we retraced our steps to the right thoroughfare."[48]

THE ESCAPE.—WADING A MOUNTAIN STREAM AT MIDNIGHT.

Image of Thomas Wolfe's epic escape with his companions from a Confederate prison (The Secret Service, the Field, the Dungeon, and the Escape, 1865, opposite page 471)

Thomas eventually made it back to Frances and his children in Mystic on his 34th birthday—January 20, 1865. He recuperated and went back to sea. He lost another vessel, the steamer *Loyalist*, while on the way to New Orleans—but all hands were saved.

Frances and Thomas moved to Galveston, Texas, with their daughter Emma so Thomas could work as a harbor pilot (one son remained in Mystic to continue his education and the other was already out to sea). Frances may have thought her worries for her husband were over as he was sticking closer to home in his new position as a pilot.

On Monday, November 8, 1875, the steamer *City of Waco* arrived in Galveston from New York and anchored offshore until conditions were more favorable for docking at the wharf. According to author Andy Hall, when a ship arrived off port, the master signaled for a pilot (using a flag signal) to come out to the ship to guide it in. Hall stated in an interview, "The pilot comes out in a pilot boat—probably a small schooner in Wolfe's case—and goes on board the larger ship and stays aboard until it arrives at the intended wharf or anchorage."

The *New York Times* (Nov. 11, 1875) reported the events that began to unfold just after midnight during the storm on November 9 at 12:30 a.m. A mate from the steamer *Abdiel*, anchored nearby, said the *City of Waco* "appeared to be one mass of flames...he heard cries of distress from five or six persons in the water. One was the voice of a woman or child clinging to what appeared to be a spar or piece of one of the vessel's masts… but every soul had been washed off of it… The mate states that the fire on the Waco seemed to spread over the entire vessel in a few minutes. He thinks she was first struck by lightning, which ignited the oil on board and burned everything on the upper decks before the passengers and crew could have left their berths and reached the small boats…Mallory & Co. [the shipping line that owned the *City of Waco*], refused to give for publication a list of the city of Waco's cargo, but acknowledged that a part of it was kerosene oil…"[49]

It was said that Captain Wolfe was "one of the best pilots in these waters"[50] and that the captain was an old seaman fully acquainted with those waters. It was thought that if lifeboats had been launched they would have been successfully handled by the experienced seamen, "though on the other hand, there are difficulties to be met that no human power can surmount."[51]

According to the inquest, Wolfe's body was found two miles away with "a small knife, all of the blades broken out, and several cuts on the legs of the deceased near the top of his boots, giving the impression that the deceased used the knife in endeavoring to cut off his boots…"[52] It was determined that the cause of death was drowning.

After a Galveston memorial service for Wolfe, packed with mourners singing hymns such as, "Shall we gather at the river?" Wolfe's body was retrieved from the undertaker's office by fellow Masons and marched to a steamer where it was met by Frances and Emma. His body was shipped to Mystic for burial alongside the Mystic River—a fitting place for a man of the sea.

Despite her anguish, Frances's spirits were lifted by the outpouring of love from the Galveston community. She published the following note of thanks in their newspaper: "…my most grateful acknowledgements to the kind friends, who…have presented me with the handsome donation of fourteen hundred dollars, as a tribute of respect to the memory of my beloved husband…and of their sympathy for myself and fatherless children. I would be glad if I could give elegant expression to my appreciation of this kindness; but I can not. My heart is too full for utterance. I can only ask God's blessing and protection to them and theirs."[53]

Only months after this disaster, Frances was struck with another heavy blow. Her sister, Ann, died when out to sea with her husband, Captain Charles Sisson (Captain Wolfe's gold seeking companion). On the day of Ann's death, Captain Sisson wrote in his journal, "During the afternoon my Dear Wife gradually grows weaker…I could see a great change in her face." Sisson records that at the end, Ann said, "God help You and the Dear Children…"[54] The following day, Saturday, May 13, 1876, after commenting on the weather at sea, Sisson writes that Ann is "gone never to return and is I trust in Heaven free from pain and sorrow. Never can I forget the closing scene…"[55] On May 26: "How I long to see the end of this unfortunate voyage."[56] On June 4: "It is one month today since my Dear Wife had her first [two illegible words] which she only survived for 8 days… she is now at rest and I am left to toil on for a while longer."[57] According to the *Norwich Courier* (July 5, 1876), Ann's preserved body arrived home to Mystic, Connecticut, by steamer from Liverpool. Charles followed on a later steamer.

Ann was buried in Lower Mystic Cemetery. Her marker is engraved with a ship stating she died at sea on the *Jeremiah Thompson*, with the coordinates giving the spot, along with these tender words: "Her smile once filled our home with gladness."

When Ann had cried, "God help You and the Dear Children" before she died, little did she know that help for her husband and motherless daughters would come from her sister Frances.

Widow Frances Wolfe married her sister's husband, Captain Charles Sisson, on March 9, 1878, combining his four daughters with her three children, making first cousins also stepbrothers and stepsisters. A month after Frances and Charles Sisson were married, Charles returned to sea.

Frances settled into the home her sister had once shared with Captain Sisson at 12 West Mystic Ave in Mystic. Typical of New England maritime communities in that era, the house has a "widow's walk" on the flattened portion of the roof. This outdoor balcony serves as a lookout over the Mystic River. According to maritime folklore, this architectural feature became known as a widow's walk because it is from this vantage point that worried wives watched for their husband's long-awaited return from sea. It was the spot from where many maritime disasters were witnessed when ships ran aground close to shore.

The "widow's walk" pictured in 2012 on 12 West Mystic Avenue, Mystic, Connecticut, sits on the home once occupied by Ann Sawyer Sisson, then by her sister, Frances Sawyer Wolfe Sisson.

It is unknown if Frances's daily routine included climbing the stairway to the attic and then to the additional few steps to the widow's walk to look for Sisson's return. Certainly Frances would have climbed up to the widow's walk if putting out a chimney fire—another purpose for this architectural feature. (One recent owner of the house said she and her husband enjoyed entertaining guests on the widow's walk because of its spectacular view.)

After nearly eight years of marriage, Charles died at home on February 27, 1885, at the age of 58. He was buried beside Frances's sister, his first wife Ann, at Lower Mystic Cemetery. Charles's marker bears the same ship as Ann's and is etched: "The voyage is ended."

Was Frances as loved by Charles as Ann was? The wording of his will seems to suggest she was: "I bequeath to my beloved wife Frances Jane Sisson the dwelling house and lot in the village of Mystic River." He also indicated that before dividing his remaining estate among his children, Frances's funeral expenses were to be paid and a "suitable memorial" was to be erected.[58]

Frances lived for another 31 years in her home with the widow's walk. Surely she must have climbed those stairs to the roof to gaze out at the waters and recall her worrisome life as the wife of two sea captains.

On September 4, 1916, Frances died at the age of 83. She is buried beside her first husband, Thomas Wolfe, along the Mystic River in Elm Grove Cemetery.

End Note: When Frances Wolfe Sisson died, the tragedy of the *City of Waco* could no longer haunt her. But for maritime historians and archeologists, it became headline news again when the U.S. Corps of Engineers discovered the shipwreck in 2003. Recent hurricanes had exposed her hull and some of the contents.

This photograph is labeled "Mrs. Chas. Sisson" on the back—but is this the first Mrs. Charles Sisson, Ann Sawyer, or her younger sister, Frances Sawyer, the second Mrs. Charles Sisson? Is this the woman who cried to her husband, "God help you," as she lay dying, or is it the woman who became the answer to that prayer? If you know, please contact the Mystic River Historical Society at info@mystichistory.org. (Photograph courtesy of the Mystic River Historical Society, Inc., Mystic, Connecticut)

Author's note: For more information about Caption Charles Sisson, who I learned was my distant cousin, read my travel memoir, Mystic Seafarer's Trail. *At one point during my research, there were so many discoveries made, some on a highly personal level, that I wondered if I was meant to find this information. If so, why? To learn I had family in Mystic? To learn that Captains Sisson and Wolfe did find gold in California and buried it somewhere near my property?*

Questions for Discussion

- Being married to a man in a dangerous profession causes worry for a wife. It was true for Frances, and remains true for many modern spouses. How is grieving different for spouses who stand on a "widow's walk," waiting hopefully for a return?

- How did remarriage change Frances' life?

- Have you ever seen a widow's walk? What part of your home is your place to sit and think?

7. WILLIAM GILLETTE (aka Sherlock Holmes)

A one-woman man

Publisher's note: William Gillette was quite a popular actor. It is remarkable, I think, that he never had a romantic liaison during the many years he survived his wife. Nowadays, he would be bombarded with media attention and offers from beautiful, eligible actresses. What was it about him, or about his beloved wife, that kept him from finding a new romance?

Famous for creating Sherlock Holmes on stage, old-time actor William Gillette not only looked like the super sleuth, he also loved like him—only once, and only for a short time.

Responsible for crafting the popular image of the Sherlock Holmes we know today – complete with curved smoking pipe – Gillette not only invented the fade-out lighting effect to end a scene, but he reinvented the art of acting entirely. Believing that melodramatic gestures and declarations were unrealistic portrayals of a character, William delivered his lines naturally—as if he was saying them for the first time. As a result of his careful use of pauses and stumbling over words when speaking, critic Heywood C. Broun called William Gillette the "Father of the Modern School of Acting."[59]

William Hooker Gillette was born on July 24, 1853, into an old Connecticut family. William's father, Frances Gillette, was a U.S. Senator. William's family hoped he would become something respectable like a lawyer, but in the end, his father supported his son's passion for theater. In fact, it was his father's advice on how to deliver believable, off-the cuff lines for a speech that prompted William to rethink the art of acting.

William left the family home in Hartford at the age of 19 in 1873 to join a stock theater company. Returning home when his money ran out, his neighbor, Mark Twain (author Samuel Clemens), got William into the cast of a stage adaptation of Twain's story, *The Gilded Age*. When William wrote the play, *The Professor*, in which he planned to star, it was with Mark Twain's influence that it got staged in New York City in 1881. It was a hit.

The Marriage Years

While performing *The Professor* in Detroit in 1882, William looked out into the audience and saw her—the woman who would change his life forever. She was the beautiful, dark haired Helen Nichols. Meeting up

41

with Helen after the show, they fell in love and married shortly thereafter. William was 28 and Helen, 21.

Helen Gillette. (Courtesy of Phil Yuris; Gillette Castle State Park)

Helen loved touring with William and made each lodging a home. She ensured William ate and rested in between the grueling hours of rehearsals, traveling and performing. She also nursed him through his frequent bouts of intestinal and digestive distress, which intensified with stress.

Then, after only six years of marriage, tragedy struck. Just as the couple was about to head to the seashore so William could rest, Helen was overcome with abdominal pain. Diagnosed with peritonitis caused by a ruptured appendix, Helen was given an injection of morphine to make her more comfortable. All knew, including Helen, she would die.

William's sister, Lilly, made it to her deathbed in time and reported in a letter Helen's words to William: "—oh it seemed as if she could never have done pouring out her sweet devotion, whispering his name when she couldn't speak aloud. Once she said 'Oh it is hard to die so young.'"[60]

William held Helen's right hand until her "body's struggle to keep the soul" ended. Helen died at 2:00 o'clock in the morning on September 1, 1888. She was 28. William was a widower at 35.

Helen was laid out in the Hartford family home "wearing one of her soft white dresses with white cashmere over and under her, lace and roses everywhere."[61] She was buried in Riverside Cemetery, Farmington, Connecticut.

Life as a Widower

William's sister Lilly referred to those days as "the summer Will's life ended."[62] William's niece took care of him for a time, taking him for drives and trying to get him to eat. Students at the Miss Porter's School, located near Riverside Cemetery where Helen was buried, reported seeing William visiting Helen's grave – often.

Soon afterwards, as a result of depression and a severe intestinal illness, William left the stage for several years. In addition to retreating south to Florida and Georgia, he spend time living in an isolated cabin in North Carolina.

In these years off-stage, William turned his hand to playwriting again. According to an aunt in 1893, his "spirits 'had begun coming up from the grave.'"[63]

One way William kept Helen alive was to create characters who reflected her personality. Young actresses who looked like Helen Gillette would be cast in the roles. For years, William wrote letters to family and friends of his severe loneliness: "Say—why can't some of you fellers adopt me – I'm awfully alone."[64]

When author Sir Author Conan Doyle, who had written his first Sherlock Holmes story in the *Strand Magazine* in 1887, sold his five-act play about Holmes in 1898, Gillette received permission to rewrite it to suit himself. Wanting to meet Gillette, Doyle was shocked when he picked him up from the train station. It was as if Sherlock had stepped straight out of his pages to greet him – for there stood Gillette wearing a deerstalker hat and Inverness cape, looking precisely the way Doyle had described Holmes: "In height he was rather over six feet, and so excessively lean that he seemed to be considerably taller. His eyes were sharp and piercing... his thin, hawk-like nose gave his whole expression an air of alertness and decision..." (from *A Study in Scarlet*).

Although the hat and cape were the creation of the *Strand Magazine*'s illustrator, it was Gillette who gave Holmes the curved pipe. "Gillette realized he needed to keep his hands free while speaking his lines, but could not do the latter if he had to clench a straight pipe in his teeth. Gillette successfully substituted the curved meerschaum or calabash pipe, which became standard Holmes gear."[65] In addition, it was not Doyle, but rather Gillette who coined the famous phrase, "Elementary, my dear Watson."[66]

Although Doyle told Gillette he could do whatever he liked with Holmes' character in the play, Gillette chose Holmes to declare love to only one woman and only once – to the attractive Alice Faulkner whose powers of observation impressed him. For the next 36 years of their character/actor partnership, Holmes and Gillette remained unattached to women.

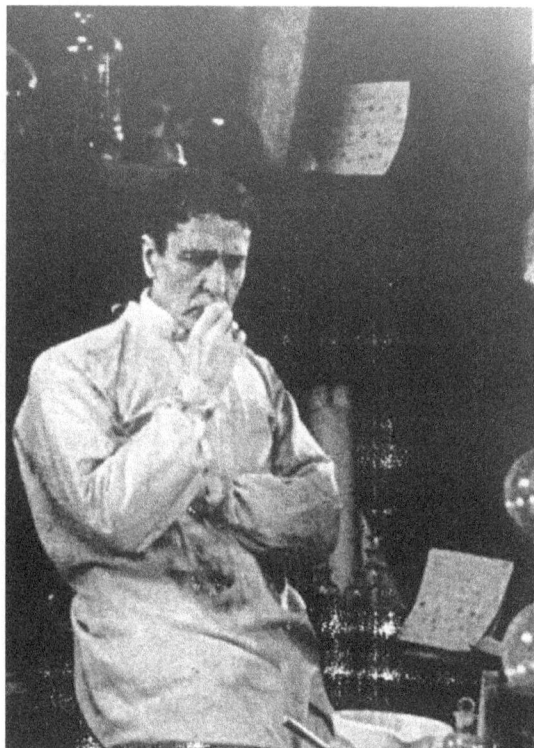

William Gillette. (Courtesy of Phil Yuris; Gillette Castle State Park)

Gillette became famous for being an eccentric, charming flirt, but other than a brief attachment to his former sister-in-law, he never formed a deep bond with a woman. Although he loved to entertain guests such as Albert Einstein and Charlie Chaplin in his retirement home, now known as Gillette's Castle, his closest relationships were with his longtime Japanese manservant, his relatives, and his hoard of cats (his cats received birthday parties on his houseboat!). When one of the young women he corresponded with fell in love with him, he told her to forget him as he had promised Helen on her deathbed he would never remarry.

William Gillette played Sherlock Holmes for the last time at the age of 82 on the radio. He died at the age of 83 on April 29, 1937, from congestive heart failure.

Buried beside his life's leading lady after a 48-year separation, William and Helen are finally able to finish their last act together.

William Gillette's marker, with figures of cats placed beside it, is pictured in 2014 at Riverside Cemetery, Farmington, Connecticut. Helen Gillette's marker is on the left.

End note: Gillette's Castle is a whimsical fieldstone fortress perched on a cliff overlooking the Connecticut River in Hadlyme, Connecticut. Listed among *National Geographic's Guide to America's Great Houses* (1999), it is riddled with the hidden rooms and passageways William Gillette designed to make a dramatic entrance or hide from unwanted guests.

Learn more about William Gillette by touring his castle and roaming the trails at Gillette Castle State Park in East Haddam, Connecticut. (860) 526-2336.

Questions for Discussion

- After Helen's death, William travelled to Florida and Georgia, finally landing in North Carolina, where he wrote. How do you feel about his roaming?

- Why do you think he wrote during this season of his life?

---

8. GEORGE PALMER PUTNAM, AMELIA EARHART

When there is no body

Pictured here in 2012 is the plaque affixed to Noank Historical Society's Latham/Chester Store, located on 108 Main Street, Noank, Connecticut, between a public beach and an oyster farming business. Earhart and Putnam were married at his mother's summer home on nearby Church Street.

Author's note: Most accounts of Earhart's life barely mention her wedding at all, except to say she got married reluctantly. The 2009 movie, Amelia, *starring Hilary Swank, showed her getting married outside—an unusual setting for an early February wedding in New England. What was the truth behind this historic event? When Mary Anderson, Curator of the Noank Historical Society, learned I was writing about Amelia Earhart's wedding, she said, "You tell everybody that the wedding scene portrayed in the movie* [Amelia] *is inaccurate. My husband's grandfather, the Groton probate judge, performed the ceremony, and my father-in-law, Robert Anderson, a young Noank lawyer at the time, attended as a witness. Before and after the ceremony, Amelia spoke to him about a new kind of aircraft she was promoting. When the judge congratulated her after the ceremony, calling her Mrs. Putnam, she replied, 'Please sir, I prefer Miss Earhart.'"*

According to the history books, Amelia Earhart was a "reluctant bride," having refused George Palmer Putnam's marriage proposals six times. She met Putnam, an arctic explorer, publicist and heir to the G.P. Putnam publishing company, in 1928 while she was employed as a social worker in Boston. At the time, George Putnam was famous as the publisher of Charles Lindbergh's book about his solo flight across the Atlantic in 1927.

George was now helping sponsors look for a woman to become the first female to fly across the Atlantic. Amelia was interviewed by the flight sponsors in New York City at the offices of G.P. Putnam's Sons Publishing Company. Upon concluding the interview in George Putnam's office, George accompanied Amelia to the train station. Shortly after returning to Boston, she received the offer to make the historic flight.

The flight took place in the trimotor Fokker, *Friendship*, previously owned by pioneering aviator and polar explorer, Richard E. Byrd. Although Amelia didn't touch the controls in her transatlantic flight with two male pilots in 1928, she nonetheless received a ticker tape parade in New York as the first woman to make it across the Atlantic by air. She found it embarrassing to receive so much fanfare when she said she felt about as useful as a sack of potatoes on the trip.

Despite her feelings about her role on that flight, she moved into George Putnam's home in Rye, New York, and wrote a book about her experiences. In the process, she became a close friend of George's wife, Dorothy Binney Putnam, and their two sons, George Jr. and David. After her book, *20 Hours 40 Minutes*, was completed, Amelia dedicated it to Dorothy Binney Putnam.

In addition to becoming close to George's wife, Amelia was also becoming close to George. Amelia said later: "Mr. Putnam and I found that we had many things in common; …We came to depend on each other, yet it was only friendship between us, or so–at least—I thought at first …"[67]

In December of 1929, Dorothy divorced George Putnam in Reno, Nevada, citing "failure to provide" and married another man the following month.[68]

George was smitten by Amelia. He brought her to visit his mother, Frances Putnam, at her vacation home in Noank, Connecticut, a seaside village in the Town of Groton. On November 8, 1930, he convinced Amelia to visit Groton Town Hall to apply for a marriage license.

CONNECTICUT STATE DEPARTMENT OF HEALTH
Bureau of Vital Statistics

Marriage License

Town of GROTON

Groom's name George Palmer Putnam 1. Bride's name Amelia Earhart
Age 42 2. Age 32
Color White 3. Color White
Occupation Publisher 4. Occupation Aviatrix
Birthplace { Town Rye, 5. Birthplace { Town Atchison,
{ State or Country N. Y. { State or Country Kansas
His residence Rye, N. Y. 6. Her residence New York, N. Y.
Single/Widower/Divorced Divorced 2d-3d Marriage 2nd 7. Single/Widow/Divorced Single 2d-3d Marriage 1st
Name of Father John B. Putnam 8. Name of Father Edwin S. Earhart
Maiden name of Mother Frances Faulkner 9. Maiden name of Mother Amy Otis
Supervision or control of Guardian or Conservator No 10. Supervision or control of Guardian or Conservator No

I, George Palmer Putnam and Amelia Earhart, the persons named in this Marriage License, do solemnly swear that the statements therein made are true, in accordance with Sec. 5263 of the General Statutes, Revision of 1918, as amended in 1921, Chap. 260, and in 1925, Chap. 260.

Sworn to before me this 8 day Dated 11/8/30. Signed Amelia Earhart
Dated 11/8/30. Signed George Palmer Putnam
Nov. 1930 Signed _____ Registrar
Judge of Probate Certificate attached

This Certifies, that the above-named parties have complied with the laws of Connecticut relating to a marriage license, and any person authorized to celebrate marriage may join the above-named in marriage within the town of Groton, Conn.

Dated November 8th 1930. Attest: Henry L. Bailey Registrar

Marriage Certificate

I hereby Certify that George Palmer Putnam and Amelia Earhart, the above-named parties, were legally joined in marriage by me at Groton (Noank) this 7th day of February 1931.

Signed Arthur P. Anderson
Official capacity Judge of Probate

Address _____

On the copy of the marriage license pictured here, Amelia listed herself as 32, a year younger than she really was. This deception began on a May 1923 aviator pilot certificate stating she was born on July 24, 1898, according to authors Elgen M. and Marie K. Long[69]. Amelia was actually born on July 24, 1897. For whatever reason, she continued to give the public, including Groton Town Hall, that younger age.

Amelia was probably very apprehensive when she entered Groton Town Hall to apply for this license. She wasn't sold on the idea of marriage in general (her parents had divorced six years earlier in 1924) [70] and had rejected other marriage proposals, including Sam Chapman's, whose proposal included the insistence that his wife not work outside the home.

According to Amelia's friends, she felt an additional reluctance to marry George Putnam because she was friends with his first wife, Dorothy.

According to author Susan Butler, Earhart was unhappy to think Putnam's feelings for her were a cause of their divorce.[71] Although Dorothy was already remarried, her divorce from Putnam was less than a year old.

At the time Earhart and Putnam applied for the wedding license, Connecticut law required a five-day waiting period from the application to the wedding. On the back of the marriage license, a typed statement from Probate Court was attached (misspelling Earhart's last name, a handwritten "a" was inserted after the "e") granting the couple permission to celebrate the intended marriage "without delay." Nevertheless, Earhart did delay.

William, the youngest son of Probate Judge Arthur Anderson, recalled his impression of the reluctant bride in a 1989 article by Larry Chick: "Amelia and George came to see my father at his house at the corner of Brook and Elm. They wanted to talk to him about the possibility of his marrying them, and I was the teenager in the way who was shooed into another room to give them some privacy. But even in the next room I heard her ask my father if she could go into his study and have a cigarette and think about marriage. When she came out, she had decided against it."[72]

Robert Anderson, another son of the judge, recalled her mood in a 1976 article by Jeff Mill. "Amelia was a little bit subdued. She just wanted to think about the whole thing more. She had dedicated herself to the business of flying, and she was anxious to retain her individuality. She was very devoted to George, there's no doubt about that. But she was afraid that changing her name somehow would diminish her stature, and she was a little upset about it." Robert added that George Putnam "was very considerate about it."[73]

The Wedding

Three months later, on Friday, February 6, 1931, George Putnam called his mother and told her that he and Amelia would be secretly driving out from New York to Noank that night. They would marry the following day, February 7, 1931.

Very few knew that Earhart and Putnam had come to Noank, but resident Clifford Sullivan, approximately 12 at the time, stated in the 1976 Mill article that when he heard the news that "Lady Lindy" was in town, it was "like trying to get into the Kennedy compound in Hyannis..." He and his friends rode up and down the street on their bicycles, "trying to get a peek of, you know, Amelia Earhart."[74]

On the day of the wedding, Putnam received a typed letter, or some would say contract, from Amelia. Her handwritten draft (available online at Purdue University Libraries), is just slightly different than the typed one he received. The handwritten draft was on Mrs. Putnam's stationary as it was printed with the words:

PHONE MYSTIC 1016
TELEPHONE NOANK
NOANK, CONNECTICUT
THE SQUARE HOUSE
CHURCH STREET

The following are excerpts from Amelia's handwritten draft:
...You must know again my reluctance to marry, my feeling that I shatter thereby chances in work which means most to me...
On our life together I want you to understand I shall not hold you to any midaevil [sic] code of faithfulness to me nor shall I consider myself so bound to you. If we can be honest about affection for others which may come to [either] of us the difficulties of such situations may be avoided...
I must exact a cruel promise and that is you will let me go in a year if we find no happiness together...[75]

There were no special wedding decorations, not even flowers. Just prior to the noon wedding, Amelia sat speaking to Robert Anderson, who was serving as a witness, on a couch in a small sitting room in the back of the yellow house.

The men wore business attire and Amelia wore a brown traveling suit, light brown blouse, shoes and stockings. George, his mother, and his uncle, were also in the room. Robert Anderson said that Amelia was "a much more attractive individual as a young woman than she was depicted...she was quite delicate looking with beautiful color and light brown hair—all in all, very attractive." He recalled that it was "quite obvious that she had become satisfied that she did want to go through with it [the wedding]."[76]

While they waited for the judge to arrive, Amelia told Robert about her desire to interest the Army and Navy in the military potential of the autogyro, a precursor to the helicopter.

When the judge arrived, Amelia was summoned to step forward for the secular ceremony. Although the *New York Times* stated that the ceremony took place in the living room while a "crackling fire burned in the fireplace," Robert Anderson remembered that his father (the judge) stood in the dining room, Earhart and Putnam stood in the passageway between the sitting room and dining room, and behind them stood George's mother and himself. Wherever the ceremony took place, all agreed it was over in less than five minutes. Robert said, "They both wanted it that way, so my father did little more than bring out the essentials of the marriage contract."[77]

The *New York Times* also added this nice touch: "As Mr. Putnam slipped a plain platinum ring on Miss Earhart's finger, the cats, coal black and playful, rubbed arched backs against his ankles."[78]

Afterwards, George's mother came over to them, placed a set of amber beads around Amelia's neck and leaned down to kiss her.[79] Preparing to leave, Judge Anderson came forward to congratulate everyone, addressing Amelia as "Mrs. Putnam."

Amelia replied, "Please, sir, I prefer Miss Earhart."

According to Robert Anderson, Jr. during a phone interview, his grandfather was unaccustomed to such "modern" airs. "My grandfather drew himself up to his full 5 feet, 8 inches, and barked, 'That service was short but effective.'"[80] With that, he left.

George Putnam called his secretary in New York to announce the wedding. There was no reception or honeymoon, and the couple was back at their desks on Monday.

Noank's historian, Mary Virginia Goodman, described the couple as "outlanders invading our little village."[81] Despite Goodman's opinion of the "outlanders," she did accommodate the request made by phone to her home the following day. She was asked if she could provide a picture of the house where Earhart had married and send it to a business in New York that sold photographs to newspapers. To fulfill this assignment, Goodman said she "obtained the services of Moses W. Rathbun, the village postmaster at the time, who was also very good with a camera..." Goodman took the roll of film, along with a photograph of Judge Anderson, which he provided, and rode the trolley to New London, Connecticut. From there, she sent the images by express to New York.[82]

When interviewed by the *New York Times* about the wedding shortly afterwards, George's mother confirmed there had been no fuss, no flowers, and the neighbors had not been notified. When the subject of flying came up, she said she had never been, and although she was afraid, she intended to fly with her daughter-in-law soon. Amelia had promised her, "I'll take you for a ride the next time I come up here."

"I'll not be afraid with her," Frances Putnam told the interviewer.[83]

The following Christmas, the couple sent Judge Anderson a card with a caricature of themselves flying together in an autogyro, which, in the sketch, looks like a small, open cockpit airplane with a propeller attached to its nose and a large one on top. A giant Santa is holding the autogyro in the air. Underneath Santa, it states:

Happy Landings!
G.P.P
A.E.[84]

Amelia and George continued to plan and promote her flying projects after their marriage. A few months after the wedding, Amelia set a world altitude record in the autogyro;[85] and in 1932, she became the first woman to fly solo nonstop across the Atlantic—a trip fraught with weather and mechanical problems. Her Lockheed Vega even went into a spin, sending her toward "whitecaps too close for comfort."[86]

Amelia said of George in an interview: "He is such a good sport about my flying. If he hadn't been I never could have made that ocean flight... he could have tried to dissuade me, or he could have whined and made it unpleasant. If he had it would have taken too much out of me. Too much nervous energy to have opposed him...but he trusted my judgment..."[87]

The Fateful Flight

In 1936, Amelia began planning an around-the-world flight, intending to take the long, dangerous route near the equator—despite the fact that several pilots had died in the attempt. Earhart's last, legendary flight occurred in a specially modified Lockheed Electra 10E, which she dubbed the "flying laboratory."

On July 2, 1937, Amelia and her navigator, Fred Noonan, disappeared somewhere over the Pacific Ocean. They were unable to find Howland Island, where they were scheduled to land for refueling. Among her last words reported to the Coast Guard cutter, *Itasca*, were: "We must be on you, but cannot see you—but gas is running low. Have been unable to reach you by radio. We are flying at 1,000 feet."[88]

In San Francisco, at Coast Guard headquarters, perspiration streamed down George's face as he paced back and forth waiting for news of Amelia and Fred. Fred's wife Bea joined him. Aggravated by her sobbing, George said to her, "It's this way Bea. One of two things happened. Either they must have been killed outright—and that must come to all of us sooner or later—or they are alive and will be picked up."[89]

After an extensive, expensive search failed to find Earhart, Noonan, and the Lockheed Electra, the government abandoned its search on July 18. George Putnam financed his own search until October 1937.[90]

Putnam publicly released a letter Earhart had given him in the event one of her flights ended in tragedy: *"Please know that I am quite aware of the hazards. I want to do it—because I want to do it. Women must try to do things as men have tried. When they fail, their failure must be but a challenge to others."*[91]

When he finally began accepting that Amelia was gone, he told Amelia's mother he was "...knocked out and was no good to myself or anyone else."[92]

Sadly, in the weeks following her disappearance, George regularly received letters Amelia had mailed along the way. He compiled her letters, articles and notes into the book, *Last Flight* (1937).

When George joined an expedition to the Galapagos for another book he was working on in December 1937, he wrote to Amelia's mother," I could enjoy it all were the circumstances different. But naturally the thought keeps recurring how AE would have enjoyed it. And there are times when the nightmare on the horizon blots out all else....Mostly the days are filled with an effort to keep from thinking. The total emptiness is appalling."[93]

In 1938, George wrote a biography about Amelia, *Soaring Wings: A biography of Amelia Earhart* (1939). It became a major source for future Amelia biographers who enjoyed anecdotes such as how Amelia rode her sled between the legs of a horse when it crossed her downhill path.

George and Amelia's mother became closer after Amelia's disappearance, but their relationship soured when he tried to establish proof of Amelia's death a year and a half after her disappearance in order to have her will probated.

Life after Amelia

On January 5, 1939, George had Amelia declared legally dead—ahead of the required seven-year waiting period. George wanted a wife, a companion. He married Jean-Marie (Jeannie) Cosigny James, a woman he met in the fall of 1938.

Upset by the marriage, Amelia's mother believed Amelia was still alive and would be found. Perhaps influenced by Amelia's mother, George's new wife, Jeannie, recalled, "I always thought there was a real possibility that [Amelia] was still alive and might come walking in the door one morning. G.P had no doubts, but he rarely talked about her...but I knew he missed her very much."[94] Jeannie divorced George in 1944 while he was serving in intelligence in World War II.

George later married Margaret Haviland. On January 4, 1950, at 63, George died of kidney failure and internal hemorrhages. His remains are at the Chapel of the Pines Crematory in Los Angeles, California. His widow received 100s of letters after his death, many stating how George inspired them to fulfill their dreams of exploration and/or writing.

The home Earhart and Putnam were married in is now a privately owned duplex. According to a 1979 article by reporter Steve Fagin, the owner celebrated her wedding anniversary annually with his friends. In her honor, they've raised their glasses to her and sung, "For She's a Jolly Good Fellow."[95]

Although most of the world believes Amelia simply ran out of fuel over the Pacific Ocean near Howland Island, there was a theory she was captured and executed by the Japanese as a spy. The authors of the book, *Amelia Earhart Lives* (1970), even suggested Amelia was alive and living under a different identity in New Jersey!

The possibility that Amelia's plane landed on a reef off the remote Pacific island of Nikumaroro is currently under investigation by The International Group for Historic Airplane Recovery (TIGHAR). In 1940, a partial skeleton of a woman matching Earhart's size and race, plus a jar the shape of an anti-freckle cream available in the 1930s, was found in the remains of a campfire under a tree on the island of Nikumaroro (Earhart was known to dislike her freckles). Had Earhart used that jar to boil water? The heel and partial sole of a woman's shoe manufactured in the 1930s, plus a box used to hold a nautical sextant (a navigational tool) were also found. Did Earhart and Noonan die as castaways? If so, how long did they struggle to stay alive, hoping for rescue?

In a 2012 article by Malia Mattoch McManus, fish and bird bones were also found[96] suggesting someone might have been marooned for months.

Although George felt the time had come to stop looking for Amelia, the rest of the world will probably keep searching.

End note: To learn more about Amelia Earhart, visit the Amelia Earhart Birthplace Museum in Atchison, Kansas. Ameliaearhartmuseum.org.

Questions for Discussion

- How do you think that not finding the body influenced George's grieving?

- George and Amelia did not have a traditional wedding reception; nor was there a typical burial service. How important is the role of ceremony in marking life passages?

- What do you think of George having Amelia declared legally dead before the end of the standard seven-year waiting period?

---

9. MILTON HERSHEY

Hershey's Kisses

Publisher's note: Though the love between Milton Hershey and his wife, Kitty, was quiet and rather private, the sweetness of the relationship is one we all share. Together, during her life, the Hershey's Kiss was developed. Many of us think that just that accomplishment would be enough. But Lisa explores how the goodness continued during the 30 years that Milton had to live without his beloved wife. Sharing both his fortune and his love made all the difference for both him and for orphans in need of a home.

Although future chocolate king Milton Hershey would one day become famous for his Kisses, he was no ladies' man. In the 1890s, those who worked with the entrepreneur at his Pennsylvania caramel factory said, "He doesn't care anything about women" and "He never bothers with the opposite sex—he never makes any more fuss over one than another."[97]

Then in 1898, the shy, rags to riches 40-year-old shocked everyone in Lancaster, including his no-nonsense Mennonite mother, when he brought home a gregarious, Irish Catholic wife from New York. The auburn-haired Catherine (Kitty) Sweeney wasn't just a wife, she was the woman who would inspire great deeds from a great man—one who would outlive her by 30 years.

Like Milton, Kitty came from humble beginnings. Milton's poverty came from several failed business ventures while Kitty's came from being the daughter of Irish immigrants. They had met a year before they married in Jamestown, New York, at a soda fountain Kitty frequented with her friends. Milton had stopped at this soda fountain called A.D. Work's Confectionery on his way to Chicago. He often traveled promoting his products and now he had a reason to keep Jamestown on his route.

Fourteen years younger than Milton, Kitty knew how to attract attention with her good looks and outgoing, joyful personality. She realized this older man with a strict religious upbringing might propose, and although she enjoyed his attentions, she was annoyed he communicated long-distance by sending telegrams instead of love letters.

Without telling his family and friends, Milton married Kitty on Wednesday, May 25, 1898, in the rectory of St. Patrick's Cathedral in New York City. He knew his mother might object because of Kitty's different religious background, but he didn't care.

He brought Kitty home by train to the house he shared with his mother, and as he predicted, they didn't "get on together at all."[98]

Mother Hershey thought Kitty was far too frivolous and vain. Milton quickly remedied the tension by buying his mother another house. Perhaps if his mother had known she would outlive Kitty by several years, she would have been happier for her son.

Although Milton didn't write love letters, he found another way to express his love for Kitty—he bought her fresh flowers every day. Whenever he traveled for business, he packed her photo in his bag (a habit that continued for the rest of his life). When Kitty thought he was away from her too long, she would call his associates and tell them to buy him a ticket home.

Kitty was a great sounding board for Milton's novel candy-making ideas. Ever a forward thinker, he became hooked on the idea of making chocolate in 1893 when he attended the World's Columbian Exposition in Chicago. There, he had watched the art of chocolate making and bought chocolate machinery, putting it in the corner of his Lancaster caramel factory. He believed caramels were just a fad, but there would always be a demand for chocolate. He said, "Chocolate is a food as well as a confection. It ought to have a big future in the United States…If I sell the caramel business I'll take the money and use it to expand my chocolate-making. I'll stake everything on chocolate."[99] Milton did later sell the caramel business.

Milton's goal was to make chocolate available to everyone, not just the rich.

Having left school before the age of 14, Milton was no scientist. He loved experimenting, however, and was determined to come up with his own chocolate formula. He didn't want to make it like the Swiss who used powdered milk. Instead, he experimented with cream, whole milk, and skim milk. He used trial and error to learn the optimum length of time to cook the batch, when to add the sugar, which cocoa beans and flavorings to use—and in what proportions. This was all done in a creamery and condensing room located on the same property as the old fieldstone farmhouse where he was born. Finally, the Hershey bar was introduced in 1900.

Kitty loved to watch Milton, whom she called her "Little Dutchman,"[100] experiment at the Homestead. Sometimes she sat for hours in a rocking chair in the kitchen regaling the women working there with her upbeat stories.

Kitty was not without troubles, however. The first signs of her serious health problems appeared three years after they were married when she began losing control of her body. Her illness was never fully diagnosed, but she had some kind of progressive muscular disease. She always remained cheerful and welcoming to all, never wanting people to feel sorry for her.

Ground was broken for Milton's chocolate factory in 1903. Milton built a town around it called Hershey with street names such as Chocolate

Avenue and Cocoa Avenue, in addition to streets named after cocoa growing regions like Ceylon and Trinidad. Milton also designed a small mansion for Kitty and himself directly across the creek from the factory. An amusement park followed later, opening in 1906. Kitty and Milton visited it on summer nights to listen to the Hershey Band. His mother disapproved of the park thinking it a frivolous distraction, but she was eventually seen in her Mennonite dress and bonnet sampling the sweets sold at the refreshment stands.

The Hershey Chocolate Company became phenomenally successful with its chocolate bars, and Milton's 1907 invention—Hershey's Kisses.

Despite their happiness, Milton and Kitty didn't have everything— they couldn't have children. Kitty was often seen stopping her carriage to give one a ride and Milton would stop whatever he was doing to find a job for any boy looking for one.

Knowing their wealth enabled them to really help these children, Kitty said, "Why don't we use it to give a home to boys who are unfortunate?"[101] So, they provided a home for boys who were either orphaned or had only one parent who was unable to support them. In 1909, the couple established the Hershey Industrial School to educate the boys.

The couple also used their wealth to travel. On one trip, Kitty planned to remain in France while Milton booked passage home aboard the luxury liner, *RMS Titanic*. He needed to return earlier than the *Titanic's* departure date, however, so took another luxury liner home, the *Amerika*, which sent a warning to the *Titanic* about large obstructions along the route. Of the 2,200 passengers and crew who left on the *Titanic* April 10, 1912, from Southampton, England, only 700 survived when it sank after striking an iceberg.

Although Kitty was spared the possibility of being widowed, three years later, it was Milton who was left widowed.

As Kitty's muscular disease continued to progress, the Hersheys found she was able to find some relief from her debilitating symptoms in the sea air, so they began spending more time in Atlantic City, New Jersey. Kitty and Milton were there in March 1915, but Milton needed to return to the business. It was planned for Kitty to return to Pennsylvania in her convertible driven by a nurse. Despite the cold, raw air, Kitty insisted on riding with the top down. By the time they reached Philadelphia, she had pneumonia. Milton was contacted and he hurried to join her.

When Kitty asked Milton for a glass of champagne, he left her side to get it. When he returned, she was dead. She died on Thursday, March 25, 1915, at the age of 43. The funeral mass was given the following Saturday in Philadelphia. Milton gave his employees the day off and a free train ticket to attend.

Milton would not let his overwhelming grief stop him from accomplishing all that he and Kitty had dreamed together. He decided to focus his fortune and energies on the school for orphaned boys. He had said of the school, "It's Kitty's idea."[102] Three years after Kitty died, he donated his entire wealth and ownership of the Hershey Chocolate Company to the school.

Milton spent the next 30 years expanding his chocolate business and improving the lives of those around him. He appeared to have no intention of falling in love again. He said, "I am very nice to little children and real old ladies, but nothing in between."[103]

As Milton aged into his 80s, he loved to sit on the roof of his mansion and tell stories about Kitty to his nurses. He would say things like "Kit used to do this" and "Kit liked it this way." He could still picture Kitty's happy and tender ways. It seemed she could still make him laugh. "Those hats...those plumes," he would reminisce.[104] He still carried her photograph with him everywhere he went.

On October 13, 1945, Milton Hershey died of a heart attack in Hershey Hospital. He is interred with Kitty in the Hershey Cemetery.

Milton Hershey will be remembered for many things—especially the school he built out of "Kitty's idea." Now co-ed and called the Milton Hershey School, it houses and educates approximately 2,000 students in grades Pre-Kindergarten through 12. It plans to grow to 2,300 students by 2020. On the school grounds you will find a statue of Milton with his arm wrapped around an orphan boy and the words, "His deeds are his monument. His life is our inspiration."

End note: To learn more about Milton Hershey, read *The Hershey Story* at HersheyArchives.org for online information. People can see what Kitty inspired in Milton with a visit to Hersheypark in Hershey, Pennsylvania. Hersheypark.com.

Questions for Discussion

- Milton did not remarry. Do you think that he and Kitty talked about that sort of thing?

- Would she have encouraged him to remarry?

- What good did Milton accomplish in the years he lived alone?

10. GRANDMA MOSES

Self-taught artist "keeps busy"

Publisher's note: Why do we love Grandma Moses so much? Is it our awe that she had the audacity to paint so late in life, with no formal training? Was it that her nostalgic scenes bring us back to a comfortable time and place? Maybe. But maybe it is because she shows that we don't have to do things perfectly to be good enough. I thank Lisa's friend, Cindy Modzelewski for encouraging her to include this wonderful American icon in this book.

When Anna Mary Moses lost her husband of nearly 40 years in 1927, the 68-year-old widow stayed busy working their farm in Eagle Bridge, New York. When her youngest son took over the farm, she devoted herself to embroidery. When arthritis made holding a needle too difficult in her late 70s, Anna Mary turned her gnarled hands to painting nostalgic scenes of farm life. She made people from over the world "feel at home" according to one German fan.[105] Becoming famous for her folksy oil paintings, the self-taught artist, dubbed "Grandma Moses" by the press, said, "The important thing is keeping busy. If I hadn't started painting, I would have raised chickens."[106]

Though receiving very little formal schooling, Grandma Moses handwrote her memories when asked about her life. Born Anna Mary Robertson on September 7, 1860, in Greenwich, New York, near the border of Vermont, she recalled the first 10 years of her life with her parents, and sisters and brothers: "…those were my happy days, free from care or worry, helping mother, rocking sister's cradle, taking sewing lessons from mother, sporting with my brothers, making rafts to float over the mill pond, roaming the wild woods, gathering flowers…"[107] Anna Mary also learned how to make soap and boil down maple sap.

At the age of 12, Anna Mary left home to earn her living as a "hired girl," living with families to help with cooking, cleaning, sewing, etc. It was in the home of her employer that she met the kind hired hand, Thomas Salmon Moses. He appreciated her cooking and she admired his thrifty ways. At the age of 27, Anna Mary married Thomas on November 9, 1887. She wore a dark green dress and matching hat with a pink feather.

The couple later moved to a 600-acre dairy farm in Virginia's Shenandoah Valley, where Anna Mary earned additional money selling butter made in molds that Thomas engraved with "Moses." She also made potato chips, which were a novelty at the time. Thomas admired Anna

Mary's practical skills, but thought her attempts at painting were "foolish." They had 10 children, five who survived infancy.

In 1905, homesick for New York, the Moses family bought a farm in Eagle Bridge, approximately 30 miles northeast of Albany, and went into the dairy business. In the winter of 1927, Thomas caught a cold fetching wood and died of heart failure on January 15. Anna Mary was 68. Before Thomas died, when he watched Anna Mary paint decorative touches to their house, he finally verbalized his admiration for her work.

When Anna Mary's youngest son and his wife eventually took over the farm, Anna Mary said she was left "unoccupied, I had to do something…"[108] And "something" she did, painting from five to six hours a day, preferring the earlier part of the day when her hands were steadier. She used leftover house paint to create cheerful images of farm life on cardboard, wood and canvas. Her studio was her bedroom, where she painted on a table, but if the painting was too big for it, she worked on her bed.

The size of her painting was determined by the size of the frame she had available from her attic or a neighbor's. She wrote, "A picture with out a fraim is like a woman without a dress."[109]

Anna Mary referred to photographs, illustrations, and her memories to create stories in paint. She liked to sit quietly to remember and imagine the past. Then she would get inspired and start painting: "Then I'll forget everything, everything except how things used to be and how to paint it so people will know how we used to live."[110] Her daughter took the paintings to the nearby drugstore in Hoosick Falls where they were displayed in the window gathering dust for a year at $3-5 per picture, depending on size.

On Easter 1938, at the age of 77, Grandma Moses was finally "discovered"—sort of. An art collector from New York, Louis Caldor, happened to be traveling through Hoosick Falls and stopped at the drugstore. Intrigued by her work, he bought all of her paintings and called on her at her home so he could buy some more. Then he drove all over with the paintings in the car, trying to interest the art community.

Louis Caldor was turned down everywhere for over a year because no one wanted to spend time and money promoting an unknown artist nearing 80—especially one whose work wasn't in the popular contemporary modern style. Caldor almost gave up until he learned of an upcoming show at the Museum of Modern Art in New York that planned to feature unknown American painters. Three of Anna Mary's paintings, including "Home, In the Maple Sugar Days," were chosen.

Nothing came of the show for several months, but Caldor encouraged Moses to continue painting and sent her "real" art materials so her pictures would look more professional. Caldor later showed her work to gallery owner Otto Kallir, an Austrian refugee from Naziism, who agreed to feature her work as "What a Farm Wife Painted" in October 1940 in New York. It was during that time that she was first referred to as "Grandma Moses" by a *New York Herald Tribune* (Oct. 8, 1940) article highlighting her advanced age.

Despite the polite but condescending comments from art critics, Grandma Moses delighted the public because she was able to convey her fond memories in paintings everyone could understand. Before the end of her exhibit, Gimbels Department Store requested her pictures for their Thanksgiving Festival on November 14. She attended the event and spoke about her work to 400 people. She recalled: "Afterwards, oh it was shake hands, shake, shake, shake—and I wouldn't even know the people now. My, my, it was rush here, rush there, rush every other place—but I suppose I shouldn't say that, because those people did go to so much bother to make my visit pleasant."[111]

Her popularity grew rapidly from there. She began receiving letters asking her to paint similar pictures for individuals. She didn't enjoy painting to fulfill an order, but she didn't like disappointing anyone either. She did not, however, like to be paid in advance as it put her under obligation.

In 1947, Hallmark acquired the right to reproduce her paintings on Christmas and greeting cards, which they did for many years, making her even more famous. In May 1949, she received the Women's National Press Club Award from President Truman for her contribution to art. She was honored along with Mrs. Franklin D. Roosevelt for her work as Chairman of the United Nations Human Rights Commission.

When Grandma Moses reflected on her success, she thought of her husband's appreciation of her work at the end of his life. "It was just as though he had something to do with this painting business."[112]

At 92, she wrote in her autobiography, *My Life's History* (published 1952): "I look back on my life like a good day's work, it was done and I feel satisfied with it. I was happy and contented; I knew nothing better and made the best out of what life offered. And life is what we make it, always has been, always will be."[113]

At 94, on June 29, 1955, when radio and television journalist Edward R. Murrow came to her home for a television interview, he asked, "What are you going to do for the next twenty years, Grandma Moses?"

Moses replied: "I am going up yonder...After you get to be about so old you can't expect to go on much farther." She explained she didn't worry about that day because "what a blessing it will be to be all united again..."

Murrow finished the interview with: "Well, you will leave more behind you more than most of us will..."[114]

Grandma Moses painted more than 1,000 pictures, 25 after she turned 100. She painted her last one in June 1961, "Rainbow." She died six months later at the age of 101 on December 13, 1961, at the Health Center in
Hoosick Falls, where she lived her final months after a fall. The evening after she died, her painting, "Mount Nebo," sold at auction for $4,000.

Grandma Moses was finally enjoying the "blessing" of being united with all who had gone before her. She is now lying beside her husband at Maple Grove Cemetery in Hoosick Falls, New York.

End note: Bennington Museum in Bennington, Vermont, houses the largest collection of Grandma Moses' paintings plus the one-room school house she attended.
Benningtonmuseum.org. 802-447-1571.

Questions for Discussion

- How did Grandma Moses respond to transitions in her life?

- What attitudes did she have that influenced how to carry on after the death of her husband?

- What hobbies do you have that might provide solace and joy for you?

11. C. S. LEWIS

A Grief Observed

Author's note: My husband and I enjoyed reading to our daughters from C.S. Lewis's "The Chronicles of Narnia." When our younger daughter passed away at 16, I found great comfort his book, A Grief Observed. *It's a book I recommend to anyone who is grieving. Lewis, who wrote it while in the depths of despair, helps us honestly express thoughts we wouldn't dare say to anyone.*

Famous for many books, such as "The Chronicles of Narnia" series, Christian author C. S. Lewis was also famous for something else: being a confirmed bachelor. He believed love had simply passed him by—as a young man and through middle age. When in his mid-50s, the Cambridge University professor told a friend he couldn't marry anyone now because it was too late for that. But then he was surprised by Joy—a Jewish mother of two who began writing him fan letters from America.

Ironically, *Surprised by Joy* was the name of Lewis's autobiography highlighting his conversion from atheism to Christianity, which was published in 1955—a year before he, at age 58, surprised himself and everyone else by marrying the outspoken New Yorker, Joy Davidman, 17 years his junior. What surprised him even more was that he fell in love—deeply. But his happiness did not last long. Joy died four years later of cancer.

Now Lewis was surprised by his grief, inspiring him to write another book, *A Grief Observed* (1961), which he began: "No one ever told me that grief felt so like fear. I am not afraid, but the sensation is like being afraid."

Mourning was not new to Lewis. Born in Belfast, Ireland, on November 29, 1898, Clive Staples Lewis, called Jack by his friends, experienced the anguish of losing his mother to cancer when he was only nine. Years later he inherited the care of another mother upon the death of a fellow soldier in WWI—something he promised he would do if his friend was killed.

During WWII, Jack and this "mother" took into their Oxford country home—called The Kilns—some of England's city children evacuated during the German bombing. This planted a seed for his first children's novel, *The Lion, the Witch and the Wardrobe*, which launched his "Chronicles of Narnia" series. *The Lion, the Witch and the Wardrobe* is about children evacuees who enter a magical world through a wardrobe owned by their host, an old professor. The inspiration for the novel occurred when a child evacuee asked Jack about his old wardrobe. She wondered if she could go inside it and if there was anything behind it.

Regarding the quality of his novel, Jack was crushed when his good friend J. R. R. Tolkien, author of *The Lord of the Rings*, told him the story had little merit. Tolkien felt joining unrelated elements such as talking animals—which Jack loved in Beatrix Potter's books—and Father Christmas didn't work. Another friend, however, whose opinion Jack also valued, encouraged him to publish it, which he did in 1950.

Meanwhile, a fan of Jack's writings on Christianity, Joy Davidman Gresham, a married writer, former communist and atheist turned Christian, asked the author of the book, *C. S. Lewis: Apostle to the Skeptics* (1949), Chad Walsh, how she could meet Jack. Walsh suggested writing to Jack as he was known to answer all letters from those seeking advice.

Jack received Joy's first letter in January 1950. He was delighted by her humor, bluntness, and intelligence. After meeting up with her in England, Jack and his brother Warren invited her to stay at their country home, where they decided to treat her like a male guest. They loved her company because she enjoyed their long treks throughout the countryside, visits to pubs for pints of beer, and made them laugh.

Joy's marriage had been difficult as a result of her husband's roving eye and battle with alcoholism. In 1954, Joy agreed to a divorce and moved to England with her boys, Douglas and David. Jack and Joy saw each other off and on as friends. However, some speculated Joy was in love with Jack. Although Jack enjoyed Joy's frank comments and observations, his friends found her to be an unappealing, abrasive New Yorker.

In 1956, Joy's visitor's visa was not renewed, meaning she needed to return to America. Although Jack still only thought of her as a good friend, he agreed to marry her on April 23, 1956, in a civil ceremony to keep her in England. They continued to live separately as nothing had changed in their relationship. But then one day, it did. In October 1956, when Joy tripped in her kitchen breaking her leg, she was diagnosed with incurable bone cancer in addition to a malignant breast tumor.

When Jack realized how desperate he was at the thought of losing Joy, he also realized something else—he was in love with her—and passionately. He engaged a minister to perform a religious marriage ceremony at Joy's hospital bedside on March 21, 1957.

Upon leaving the hospital a week later, Joy moved into The Kilns with Jack and his brother Warren. Jack prayed for a miracle. To his utter delight, Joy went into remission. Joy wrote to their friend Chad Walsh, "Jack and I are managing to be surprisingly happy considering the circumstances: you'd think we were a honeymoon couple in our early twenties..."[115]

After a belated honeymoon to Wales and to Ireland, Jack remarked to a friend, "I never expected to have, in my sixties, the happiness that passed me by in my twenties."[116]

But that happiness would not last long—Joy's cancer returned. Joy cried bitterly, "And there was so much to live for."[117]

At one point during her rapid and painful decline, Jack begged Joy: "If you can—if it is allowed—come to me when I too am on my death bed."

"Allowed!" Joy said. "Heaven would have a job to hold me..."[118] Joy made Jack promise, however, that he would "keep clear of spiritualists."[119]

Among Joy's last words to Jack were, "You have made me happy,"[120] and to the hospital chaplain, "I am at peace with God."[121]

Joy died July 13, 1960, at the age of 45. Upon her request, Jack had her cremated. Her ashes were scattered in the rose garden at the Oxford Crematorium, less than a mile from The Kilns. Jack wrote a tender poem in honor of Joy, which is etched on a plaque at the Crematorium and states that Joy was the "Loved wife of C. S. Lewis."

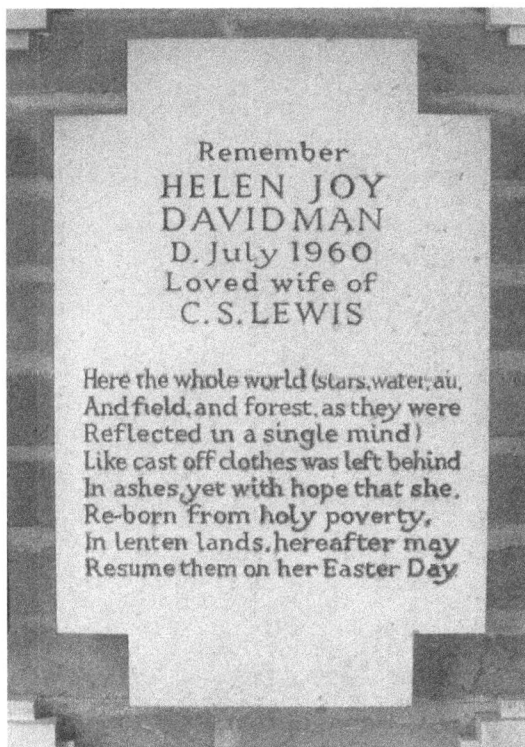

Joy's memorial poem written by C.S. Lewis pictured in 2006 at Oxford Crematorium, England. (Photograph by Stephanie Jenkins)

Jack continued to care for Joy's sons as he worked through his grief in the way he always dealt with his feelings—by writing. His raw thoughts grew into the short book, *A Grief Observed*, which was so honestly and painfully written—complete with accusations toward God—that he published it under another name. Having since been republished under his own name, he states in the opening page, "There is a sort of invisible blanket between the world and me. I find it hard to take in what anyone says." And about God he writes, "Why is He so present a commander in our time of prosperity and so very absent a help in time of trouble?"[122]

Jack only outlived Joy by three years. He died at home from renal failure on November 22, 1963, the same day U.S. President John F. Kennedy was assassinated. Perhaps Jack got his wish that day and Joy was able to come to his death bed.

C. S. Lewis is buried with his brother Warren at Holy Trinity Church, Headington Quarry, Oxford, England, where he worshipped for over 30 years. Because he gave away most of his money while he was alive, his estate was relatively small. He did, however, provide for the education of Joy's sons and for his brother Warren.

End note: A dramatization of the love between Jack and Joy, and Jack's grief after her passing, can be seen in the film *Shadowlands*, most recently released in 1993 starring Anthony Hopkins and Debra Winger.

Gravestone of C.S. Lewis and his brother Warren at Holy Trinity Church, Headington Quarry, Oxford, England. (Photograph by Mike Stranks)

The Narnia window adjacent to the "Lewis Pew" at Holy Trinity Church, Headington Quarry, Oxford, England. Installed as a memorial to a brother and sister associated with the church. (Photograph by Mike Stranks)

Questions for Discussion

- What did C.S. Lewis do after the loss of Joy that contributed to the world?

- Who benefited from his activities during widowhood?

12. NORMAN ROCKWELL

Poetic inspiration

Author's note: A highlight of my visit to Stockbridge, Massachusetts, was a film at the Norman Rockwell Museum. I was intrigued by the story of how Rockwell fell in love again after the loss of his wife. I became aware of the power of poetry – it helps people fall in love!

When Norman Rockwell entered his bedroom to alert his wife, Mary, to a phone call, he knew immediately something was wrong. She was lying abnormally still on their bed. The 65-year–old artist lost his 51-year-old wife unexpectedly that day. Earlier in that afternoon of August 25, 1959, Mary had told her daughter-in-law that she was going upstairs to take a nap.

It was said that the famous *Saturday Evening Post* illustrator was unable to discuss his loss—or his spouse. Although her death certificate said she died as a result of heart failure, some speculated she had taken an overdose of her medication. She had done so at least twice before and had been sent to psychiatric hospitals. But there was never any proof of an overdose—no missing medication or suicide note. The mother of Rockwell's three sons had appeared to be feeling well and was looking forward to the arrival of their first grandchild. The amount of drugs in her system was never known as Rockwell did not want an autopsy done. Mary was Rockwell's second wife. His first wife had left him for another man in 1930 after 14 years of marriage (there were no children from their union).

Regardless of the cause of Mary's death, after nearly 30 years of marriage, Rockwell the widower appeared ill and unfocused when seen about Stockbridge, Massachusetts, where he had moved six years earlier from Vermont. Rockwell had moved to Stockbridge, a small town set among to the Berkshire Mountains, to be closer to a leading psychiatric hospital, the Austen Riggs Center, where Mary could receive treatment. Rockwell himself sought help there as he, too, suffered from depression and a feeling of inadequacy. Rockwell's psychoanalyst, the famous Erik Erikson, became worried enough about the possibility of Rockwell committing suicide that he took away the gun Rockwell kept in his studio.

Within a year of Mary's passing, he donated $1,000 to buy children's books for the Stockbridge Public Library. Mary had been a school teacher. Rockwell himself never graduated from a traditional high school, having left it early to study art. A year after Mary's death, Rockwell began working on *The Golden Rule*, a composite of 28 faces of people from all walks of life and religions. In the top right corner, he painted the face of his Mary holding their grandson, born a few months after her death.

Erikson, Rockwell's psychoanalyst, insisted the artist get out of the house and get among people by joining a group. In October of 1960, Rockwell took a Monday night poetry class at a nearby library. In addition to smoking his pipe nonstop and disrupting the class over his amusement at the seriousness of the students when discussing the intentions of famous poets, Rockwell was falling in love. The object of his desire was his instructor, the never-before-married 64-year-old English teacher, Mary (Molly) Punderson. Upon her recent retirement from the Milton Academy, a prestigious prep school in Massachusetts, Molly had returned to Stockbridge, where her father had managed the Red Lion Inn for six decades.

Like Rockwell's late wife Mary, Molly loved literature. Apparently, Rockwell admired women who could quote passages of it. He asked Molly to join him at a play in nearby Pittsfield. As far as anyone knew, Rockwell was Molly's first male suitor.

Two years after Mary's death, at St. Paul's Episcopal Church, where her funeral was held, Rockwell married 65-year-old Molly on October 25, 1961. When people commented to Molly that she married late in life, she replied, "Norman was worth waiting 62 years for."[123] The couple went to the Plaza Hotel in Manhattan, New York, to begin their honeymoon – and the next chapter of their lives, one that would last 17 years.

Without children and grandchildren of her own to distract her, Molly set about taking over Rockwell's care—especially his schedule and finances, which freed him to concentrate, paint, and meet his deadlines on a timelier basis. Molly's wise handling of their money helped them afford several major trips a year, which helped him find the rest and refreshment he needed to face his next assignment. Although Rockwell wasn't one to sit around discussing literature with Molly, he did accompany her to classical concerts because he enjoyed watching the musicians perform.

Molly was willing to play the role of "bad guy" in the couple's personal life by insisting his friends and family limit unscheduled interruptions so Rockwell could paint—which he did seven days a week in his studio. Molly insisted his daily schedule include a nap and their 4.7-mile bike ride together throughout Stockbridge. In the evenings, they relaxed in the gazebo they built in a private area of their yard—away from the prying eyes of fans and friends who strolled by. In their gazebo, Norman enjoyed a hot toddy and Molly, a gin and tonic. She dressed every day for Norman as if they were going out to dinner.

With Molly as his inspiration, Rockwell wrote and illustrated his only book specifically for children – *Willie Was Different: A Children's Story*. Originally written in 1967, it was about a skinny wood thrush named Willie whose life was forever changed when he heard a flute being played at an open window by an elderly, spinster-looking librarian. Filled with joy at her playing, the wood thrush sang along with her, making up his own variations. The librarian, having never been accompanied by a bird before, was enchanted by Willie so they played duets together. News of Willie's genius reached bird experts who insisted he be brought to the city where he could be celebrated by all. Though the librarian worried he would be unhappy, she agreed and took him there by train. But Willie didn't like this bustling new location – he was unable to eat, sleep or sing anymore.

Many believe Rockwell's children's story is autobiographical—everything from the sketch of the skinny wood thrush to the elderly librarian whose name is Miss Polly (one letter different from Molly). At the end of the story about the gifted yet unhappy Willie in the big city, Miss Polly brings Willie back to the quiet of their woods so he can find rest. The story concludes with, "Very softly, just for themselves, Willie and Miss Polly, his true old friend, brought to life the songs they had created together."

When Norman became too frail for the couple's daily bike ride in his 80s, Molly took him for car rides. Near the end of his life, dementia gradually came to call. Except to attend her church activities on Sunday, Molly kept her husband company in his bedroom when he became too ill to leave it.

Rockwell died of emphysema at the age of 84 on the evening of November 8, 1978. He was buried in Stockbridge Cemetery beside Mary. Molly, who died six years later in 1985, was buried on his other side.

For a man celebrated for his ability to tell us stories with his paintings—some nostalgic, others with social impact—his simple headstone tells us very little. The front merely says "Rockwell."

The back of Rockwell's stone states:

NORMAN ROCKWELL
FEBRUARY 3, 1894 – NOVEMBER 8, 1978
HIS WIFE
MARY RHODES BARSTOW
NOVEMBER 26, 1907 – AUGUST 25, 1959
HIS WIFE
MARY PUNDERSON (MOLLY)
SEPTEMBER 15, 1896 – JULY 20 1985

End note: For more information about Norman Rockwell, visit the Normal Rockwell Museum in Stockbridge, Massachusetts.
nrm.org, (413) 298-4100.

Questions for Discussion

- Literature was a theme in Norman's marriages. When seeking a new romance, what traits would you seek in a new partner?

- Do you think Norman's last marriage improved his life? How?

- Norman honored Polly's memory by donating to the library. How could you honor the memory of a loved one's life?

13. CAPTAIN VON TRAPP

A stepmother for his children

Author's note: I remember the thrill of seeing The Sound of Music *for the first time with my grandmother, Gertrude Avazian, when I was five years old. Was Georg von Trapp truly as stern as the movie portrayed before he married Maria? I couldn't wait to research his life to find out which parts of the movie were true—and which were not.*

Many know Maria von Trapp from the 1965 movie *The Sound of Music* starring Julie Andrews, but the film reveals little of widower Captain von Trapp before he met Maria at his Austrian villa in 1926.

Just as in the movie, when Maria, a 21-year-old candidate at the Abbey of Benedictine Nuns, was called into the Reverend Mother's office in October 1926, she thought she was in trouble. She was the "black sheep" of the community, often scolded for infractions such as sliding down the banister or whistling inappropriately. Raised by relatives after the death of her mother when she was two, Maria said her upbringing was "more that of a wild boy than a young lady."[124]

Instead of scolding Maria for another infraction, the Reverend Mother said the doctor thought Maria's ever worsening headaches were from leaving her life of mountain exercise for a sedentary existence behind the convent's cloistered wall. It appeared to the Reverend Mother that it was God's will for Maria to leave the convent for nine months to tutor the sickly daughter of Baron von Trapp, a national hero and retired captain of the Austrian Navy. The little girl was left too weak from scarlet fever to walk the three miles to school with her siblings. She was one of the seven children left motherless when Captain von Trapp's wife, Agatha, died four years earlier.

Although sick at heart to leave the convent, Maria believed wholeheartedly the lesson taught there: "The only important thing on earth for us is to find out what is the will of God and to do it."[125]

Carrying her guitar and wearing ill-fitting, hand-me-down clothes, Maria hopped on a bus to the captain's large estate. Just as in the movie, Georg von Trapp called the children to meet Maria using his brass whistle, but they weren't being raised in a harsh, militaristic way. Their father was just a sad, 46-year-old man who felt shy with his children. He rarely stayed home because they reminded him of their mother.

Born April 4, 1880, Captain von Trapp earned his first decoration fighting in the Boxer Rebellion in China. Fascinated by the potential of a submarine in warfare, he was given command of one of the first submarines in the Austrian Navy. The beautiful, wealthy young lady who christened it, Agatha Whitehead, was the granddaughter of the inventor of the torpedo, Robert Whitehead. Georg fell in love and they were married soon afterwards. Their happiness was shattered by the outbreak of WWI. Georg found his experimental submarine challenging – exhaust gases poisoned the crew and the periscope couldn't be lowered and raised independently so the whole boat had to move with it. Nevertheless, Georg cleared the Adriatic Sea of enemy ships and earned several medals, including the highest one—the Cross of Empress Maria Theresa. This raised Georg to the baronetcy.

When Austria lost the war, it also lost its seacoast. Georg was now a captain without a ship—and without a successful vocation. Only Agatha made this bearable. By 1921, they had seven children. In 1922, Agatha died during an epidemic of scarlet fever. Finding their home filled with painful memories, they moved to an estate in Salzburg.

Georg hired several female staff to care for his children, but his relatives persuaded him to find just one woman – a new wife. It was expected that he would become engaged to Princess Yvonne. Maria prayed nightly for the captain: "Dear Lord, send him a good wife who will be a good mother to his dear children, and let him be happy from now on."[126]

Although Maria was only in charge of young Maria, she included all of the children in singing lessons and jaunts throughout their estate. Georg began to enjoy staying home and played his violin to join them when they sang.

The children now felt they had their second mother. Much to Maria's horror, Georg told Princess Yvonne he couldn't marry her because he was in love with someone else – Maria. But Maria wanted to become a nun! Asking Reverend Mother what she should do, she was heartbroken when she replied that it was the will of God for Maria to marry the Captain and be a good mother to his children.

Wearing edelweiss in her bridal veil, Maria married Georg on November 26, 1927. She eventually grew happy in her life with Georg and gave birth to two daughters. Then, Georg was hit with a major blow—the financial institution which housed the majority of his funds went bankrupt. Devastated by what that meant for their children, Georg found Maria's delight at this turn of events unnerving—she believed God was preparing something exciting for them as a family.

To earn money, they converted a room in their home into a chapel and took in a priest as a border. Singing daily for the Holy Mass, they now took their music seriously. The priest insisted they learn proper technique and conducted their rehearsals. According to Maria, though they didn't realize it yet, "This was the birth of the TRAPP FAMILY SINGERS."[127]

When Maria and the children were overheard rehearsing outside by the famous singer Lotte Lehmann who came to inquire about renting their home, Lehmann said, "You must not keep that for yourselves, that precious gift. You must give concerts…you have to go to America!"[128]

When Georg learned the singer wanted to book his family the following day for a singing contest, he was mortified. Maria recorded his words in her memoir: "'Madam, that is absolutely out of the question,' he said, and meant it."[129] It was highly improper for an aristocratic family to perform publicly. He finally relented, however, giving into Maria's belief that it was God's will, but couldn't bear the outcome—his family won first prize.

On March 11, 1938, Austria was invaded by Hitler. The von Trapps were becoming unfavorably noticed by the Nazis—their daughter wouldn't raise her hand to the Heil Hitler in school and they didn't hang the Nazi flag on their home. Then came three temptations, ones that would end their dire financial struggles but test all that Georg stood for. He received an invitation from Hitler's Navy Department to command a new submarine; their son was offered a medical position; and his family was asked to sing for Hitler's birthday. Georg explained to his family that if they accepted money and praise from the Nazis, "then we shall have to give up the spiritual goods: our faith and our honor. We can't have both anymore."[130] The family agreed they must refuse the invitations. Saying no to Hitler was dangerous, so they knew they had to leave their home and country.

In the summer of 1938, with nine children and one on the way, the von Trapps left Austria by train toward Italy under the pretense of mountain climbing. They later boarded a boat for the U.S. The very day they left Austria, the border was closed and nobody could leave.

When they arrived in America, all they had between them were some suitcases and $4.00. Though their transition into American ways and escalators was difficult, the family learned to love the country that didn't ask "Who are you?" but rather, "How good are you?"[131]

The von Trapps felt most at home in the mountains of Vermont where they bought an old farm in Stowe and started a music summer camp. Maria believed that anyone over 50 could overcome a lack of musical training by taking up the recorder. Meanwhile, they worried about their two sons who were serving their new country in Italy during the war.

With WWII over in the summer of 1945, their sons returned home and their Austrian estate was returned to them, which they sold. During the war, it had been confiscated by Heinrich Himmler and visited by Hitler. While there, Hitler ordered several soldiers gunned down because one was humming a Russian folksong.

The von Trapps sent donations, raised during their concerts, to their former countrymen to help in their recovery.

While on their annual concert tour across the U.S. in 1947, Georg told Maria he didn't feel well. Diagnosed with advanced lung cancer, he and Maria returned to Vermont.

Maria wrote of that time: "He liked it best when I sat at his bedside, held his hand, and read aloud to him. Sometimes he fell asleep during the reading; then with my left hand I got out my rosary. It was strange: Georg, who was always so concerned for others and never claimed a service for himself, now did not want to let me out of his sight for a minute."[132]

Georg died on May 30, 1947, at the age of 67. Maria was a widow at 42 after 19 years of marriage—and she was pregnant, but lost the baby soon afterwards.

Maria performed her responsibilities at their music camp as if she were a machine. "You repeat over and over again: 'Thy Will be done.' But what you feel is terrible emptiness. The sun has set in your life; it is getting cold. The hundreds of people around you cannot console you for the loss of the one."[133]

Maria published her memoir, *The Story of the Trapp Family Singers*, in 1949. She began welcoming guests to the family's rustic home/lodge in Stowe the following year. In 1956, the Trapp Family Singers performed their last concert in the U.S. In 1964, during the shooting of *The Sound of Music* in Salzburg, Maria visited while they were filming the song, "I Have Confidence." Upon her request, the costume department outfitted Maria and her granddaughter in period costumes and they can be seen behind Julie Andrews when she walked through an arch toward the fountain.

Four decades after Georg's death, Maria died on March 28, 1987. She was 82. They are buried at the family cemetery at the Trapp Family Lodge.

End note: Maria and Georg's youngest child, Johannes von Trapp, born shortly after they arrived in the U.S., is currently the president of the Trapp Family Lodge, which they call "A mountain resort in the European tradition." Learn about their lodge and family at: www.trappfamily.com, 1-800-826-7000.

Maria von Trapp's grave marker pictured in January 2016 in the family plot at the Trapp Family Lodge in Stowe Vermont. (Photograph by Joanne Z. Moore)

Questions for Discussion

- Have you ever considered *The Sound of Music* from the Captain's point of view?

- What do you think of the risks he took in defying Hitler?

- How did a second marriage influence his life?

14. GEORGE BURNS

The show must go on

Gracie Allen's crypt front is pictured in 2001 at Forest Lawn Memorial Park, Glendale, California. (Photograph by Connie Nisinger)

Publisher's note: Three generations have known and loved George Burns. But none of us knew and loved him like Gracie Allen did. Here is a little glimpse backstage, and into their private life. While he may not have been a perfect husband, the favor of Gracie's forgiveness just made him love her more. Lisa explores how George managed his life after his loss, and how he worked to memorialize her.

Actor George Burns lost the love of his life at 68 when wife and co-star Gracie Allen died of a heart attack in 1964. Despite outliving her for 32 years, he never remarried – but he didn't sit around either.

    A performer since the age of eight, Burns knew what had to be done after Gracie died: the show must go on. He went on to win his first Oscar at age 80 in the film, *The Sunshine Boys* (1975). He played God in the film, *Oh God!* (1977), then its two sequels, and he was even determined to appear on his 100th birthday on January 20, 1996, at Caesar's Palace in Las Vegas. Burns said, "I can't die—I'm booked."[134]

In Burns' mind, however, his "show" did not go on without Gracie. He regularly visited her vault in Glendale, California, to discuss things with her. "I don't know if she hears me, but I do know that every time I talk to her, I feel better," he said in his memoir, *Gracie: A Love Story* (1988), which he finally wrote at 92. Burns regretted waiting nearly 25 years after her death to write it. In his acknowledgements, Burns wrote: "How could I have put off what turned out to be such a rewarding and somehow comforting experience for me?"[135]

Burns even told Gracie about the book. "I go to Forest Lawn Cemetery once a month to see her and I tell her everything that's going on. I told her I was writing this book about her. Evidently she approves— she didn't say anything."[136]

Reminiscing, Burns said, "I lie a lot. That's the truth. But usually, when I tell a lie, I admit it. I'm a very honest liar. But when I talk about Gracie I don't lie. I don't have to. The truth is unbelievable enough."[137]

The book's opening line is typical Burns: "For forty years my act consisted of one joke. And then she died."[138]

He didn't find his one "joke" until he was 27. Until then, Burns performed with little success during the heyday of vaudeville, a popular style of entertainment in the late 1800s/early 1900s. Not considered "legitimate theater," vaudeville combined several unrelated songs, dances, and comedy acts.

Unlike Gracie, George Burns, born Nathan Birnbaum, was not from a family of performers. Rather, he was the son of a kosher butcher shop helper and part-time synagogue cantor. Born on January 20, 1896, on the Lower East Side of Manhattan, Burns was one of 12 children left behind when his father died at 47 during an influenza epidemic.

Burns earned money shining shoes and delivering papers, and at eight, got a job at a candy store mixing chocolate and cherry syrups. Working with two other boys in the basement, they sang in harmony to amuse themselves—and that was where Burns was "discovered." When a local postman stopped in to order a soda, he overheard the boys, "booked" them on street corners, and passed a hat to collect money. Burns quit school at age 10 to work full-time. He struggled along as a second-rate "song and dance" man.

At 25, he still received the lowest spot on the bill and had no act of his own. As a dancer, he would always need a partner. He joked that he briefly married Hanna Siegal because her parents would only let her accept a 26-week tour if they were married.

In the winter of 1923, George's luck changed. He met the beautiful, Irish Catholic Grace Allen from San Francisco who came back stage after a performance looking for a new show partner. George loved her eyes—especially because they were two different colors. Despite her high-pitched voice, she could sing as well as dance and act. She appeared elegant in the long sleeves or high gloves she always wore to cover burns down her left arm. She had received these scars from the hot oil of a knocked over kerosene lamp.

George decided to become a comedian. He told Gracie they would perform a flirtation act. She would play the "straight" man feeding him lines that he could return with a joke. When they debuted in Newark, New Jersey, Gracie came onstage in a conservative dress and high heels, whereas George wore shortened trousers and an upturned hat so people would know he was funny. Despite these visual clues, however, their meager audience got it wrong—they laughed at Gracie's lines instead of George's!

Never one to argue with an audience, Burns quickly rewrote the script before the next show to give Gracie some of the funny lines. He said, "It broke my heart but I was young and hungry and not a dope."[139] Despite Gracie's intelligence offstage, she would play a sweet, sincere "dumb girl" onstage.

By the second show, Burns knew they had a hit. The audience felt protective of Gracie, who didn't appear to know she was funny. George determined that he should never belittle her character—not even when her lines called for her to believe she was saving electricity by using a short electric cord on her vacuum cleaner.[140]

They signed on to the vaudeville circuit as a standby replacement act for "no shows." Keeping their bags packed, they were often on a bus or train at a moment's notice.

George was falling in love with Gracie. Gracie, however, got engaged to her Irish dancer boyfriend Benny Ryan who was often on tour elsewhere. It took George almost a year before he could tell Gracie how he felt about her. She, however, did not reciprocate his feelings.

By 1924, George and Gracie were receiving regular bookings. Despite Gracie's battles with migraine headaches, she, like George, believed "the show must go on" and performed no matter what. Burns began using a cigar as a prop to give him something to do with his hands. He continued to refine their act:

GEORGE: Did the maid ever drop you on your head when you were a baby?

GRACIE: Don't be silly George. We couldn't afford a maid. My mother had to do it.[141]

Despite their growing success, Gracie wanted to quit the show to marry her fiancé. In 1925, George began proposing to Gracie. He told her his Orthodox Jewish background wouldn't be an obstacle because she could raise their children Catholic. George recalled, "So my mother approved of my marrying Gracie, and Gracie's mother approved of my marrying Gracie; the one who objected was Gracie."[142]

Finally fed up with the strain of wondering what was going to happen with Gracie, a week before Christmas 1925, George gave her an ultimatum—she had to agree to marry him in 10 days, or they had to part ways. When Gracie failed to call her fiancé, Benny Ryan, on midnight of Christmas Eve 1925 as they agreed, Benny phoned her shortly after midnight. When he asked why she hadn't called, "Don't you love me anymore?" Gracie replied that she didn't think she did.[143]

At 3 a.m. on Christmas morning, Gracie called George Burns and told him she would marry him. They were married a few weeks later on January 7, 1926, by the justice of the peace while on tour in Cleveland, Ohio. When the newlyweds reached Syracuse, New York, they were thrilled to see their names in lights on the marquee:

"THE ORPHEUM WELCOMES
MR. AND MRS. GEORGE BURNS"[144]

Though they wanted children, they were unable to have them, so they adopted a girl and a boy.

The couple's continued success eventually led to *The George Burns and Gracie Allen Show* in 1950, which became one of the top-rated television shows of the decade.

In the early 1950s, Gracie suffered her first heart attack. She found performing very wearying, but Burns talked her into performing another season, then another. He believed he just didn't have an act without Gracie. In February 1958, however, she was just too exhausted and announced her retirement.

Gracie died of heart failure in 1964. George felt a lot of remorse over urging Gracie to continue the show for as long as she did. Beside himself and unable to sleep, George finally found some relief: "My life was Gracie. But then, about two months later, I started sleeping in her bed—we had twin beds—and things just started turning around for me."[145] George began sleeping peacefully, feeling that Gracie was with him in spirit.

In addition to regretting asking Gracie to work for so long, George regretted something else: "I made one big mistake that I've never talked about before. I cheated on Gracie once."[146] Although he turned down many a starlet, including Marilyn Monroe, he slipped in the early 1950s.

Gracie found out about it, but said nothing. He knew she knew, and in his appreciation for her silence, he bought her an expensive silver centerpiece she wanted—something he had said no to prior to the affair. Seven years later, while Gracie was out shopping and saw another expensive silver centerpiece, she remarked to a friend, "You know, I wish George would cheat again, I really need a new centerpiece."[147]

George never forgot Gracie's forgiveness. "My mistake could have ruined both of our lives...If she had decided to make a big deal about it, we might not have had another decade together...So today I think about Gracie every single day...And the other girl, the starlet, I wouldn't even recognize her if I ran into her. That's how smart Gracie really was."[148]

In George's 84th year, the *Reader's Digest* article, "'Oh God!' It's George Burns!" indicated that George was just as kind and gentle as he appeared in his onscreen characters. George said, "It takes just as much energy to be rotten as to be nice."[149] About his religion, though not practicing formally, George said, "I believe in God. I believe that God is in every person and therefore I don't get angry with people and I don't hate people. If something bad happens—I forget right away."[150] Joking that part of his longevity was a result of smoking cigars—about 15 a day—he said,. "Three doctors told me to stop the cigars years ago. Of these three, two are already dead—and the third one has been coughing a lot lately."[151]

At age 92, George told *People* magazine that he was not afraid of death because, "I know Gracie's up there. And if they've got vaudeville, we can be headliners."[152]

Although George lived to his 100th birthday on January 20, 1996, he was too ill to keep his engagement in Las Vegas. He died on March 9, 1996, and is interred with Gracie. Their marker reads: "GEORGE BURNS AND GRACIE ALLEN—TOGETHER AGAIN."

Questions for Discussion

- How did George use humor, both during Gracie's life and after her death?

- How do you think his use of humor influenced his listeners?

- What do you think of how George and Gracie managed his episode of infidelity?

15. KATHARINE GRAHAM

Takes the reins of the *Washington Post*

Katharine Graham pictured in 1986. (Photograph courtesy of Graham Holdings)

Publisher's note: When I first read the memoirs of Katharine Graham, I felt an affinity for her. We both started as women in traditional roles, and then the world changed around us. So she was first my feminist role model, assuming a responsible position in a previously male dominated world. She then led the way for me as I rebuilt my life after the loss of my husband. She demonstrated core values that I share: care for families combined with competence in the greater world. I loved her honest humility as she began to work outside the home, and am inspired by her willingness to take a risk and by her determination to learn.

When Katharine Graham's husband, Philip Graham, publisher of *The Washington Post* ended hislife, Katharine went to work. Thinking she would just keep the *Post* in the family until her children could take over, little did the shy housewife know she would face off with the government and bring the *Post* into a new era of investigative journalism by doing what she thought was right—printing the truth.

At 80 years old, Katharine's truth also earned her a Pulitzer Prize for her best-selling 1997 autobiography, *Personal History*. Katharine said, "I don't suppose that I meant to tell everything to everybody. But once I sat down to write my story, I tended to be frank and open. I wanted to be very truthful. I wrote it the way I saw it, and the way the research [went]."[153] The book was praised for her honesty about her husband's mental illness, her changing views on a women's role in society, and major news events that affected the direction of the paper.

Katharine Meyer Graham was born in New York on June 16, 1917, and moved to Washington, D.C. soon after. Katharine's father, Eugene Meyer, made big money on Wall Street and bought the struggling *Washington Post* in 1933 when Katharine was 16. Katharine went off to Vassar College, transferring two years later to the University of Chicago. In 1939, she went to work at the *Post* editing letters to the editor. She met Philip Graham, a lawyer and a clerk at the Supreme Court, through mutual friends. The two married on June 5, 1940. They suffered immediate tragedy with the loss of their first baby (due to a hospital accident), but went on to have four more children.

Although the *Post* had made strides in circulation and advertising under her father, it was still losing money every year. Wanting a successor to the paper, Katharine's father offered it to Philip, who was 30 at the time. After some thought, Philip accepted the work. Soon thereafter, Katharine's father left the paper for a position as president of the World Bank. Philip was named publisher at age 31, and from 1947, he, too, struggled to make the paper profitable.

In the meantime, Katharine took full charge of home matters, handling everything so Philip could concentrate on the high demands of the paper. In addition to the stress of the business, Philip also battled undiagnosed manic-depression before proper drugs were available or advised for it. Although he admitted himself into a psychiatric hospital, on a weekend out in August 1963, he killed himself with a rifle at their Virginia home.

Katharine was widowed at 46 with four children, the oldest 20. The family's political connections were such that the funeral took place in the Washington National Cathedral with President Kennedy in attendance. Kennedy sent her a note telling her how helpful Philip had been to him since his arrival in Washington. Jackie Kennedy wrote Katharine an eight page letter—"one of the most understanding and comforting of any I received."[154]

Of her new widowhood, Katharine wrote in her memoir, "Left alone, no matter at what age or under what circumstances, you have to remake your life…Always in my mind was the climax of the years of secret struggle with Phil's illness, the shock of the suicide, the loss, and the eternal questions about why and what next."[155]

A month after his suicide, Katharine went to work. She was elected President of The Washington Post Company on September 20, 1963, and set about learning the business. In her mind, she would just observe, remaining a "silent partner" until her children could take over. "I didn't understand the immensity of what lay before me, how frightened I would be by much of it, how tough it was going to be, and how many anxious hours and days I would spend for a long, long time. Nor did I realize how much I was going to enjoy it all."[156]

Though Philip and her father had discussed their work at the paper with Katharine, she felt overwhelmed without Philip's guidance. "Though I had learned a great deal from him, I still felt insecure making my own decisions."[157] But one thing Katharine did know—she had inner strength gained during her last demanding year with Philip when forced to bear all the burdens of home.

Katharine finally realized she just couldn't lead the *Post* the way Philip or her father had done. She could only do the job in her own way— whatever that way turned out to be. In addition to her outstanding staff, she knew she had another, very important asset—her passion for the business. "I cared a great deal about the company…It'd been part of my whole life…"[158]

Katharine wrote in her memoir: "What I essentially did was to put one foot in front of the other, shut my eyes, and step off the edge."[159]

Some of her simplest new duties terrified her—having to speak before groups. "I was asked to go down and say "Merry Christmas" at the company lunch…I practiced making this speech saying "Merry Christmas" in front of the children, because I'd never said anything in public."[160]

Katharine was named publisher of the paper in 1969. In the early 1970s, Katharine would have to do a lot more than say, "Merry Christmas." In 1971, while the federal government fought against *The New York Times* to prevent publication of the "Pentagon Papers," which contained secrets about its handling of Vietnam, it was up to Katharine as publisher to decide if *The Washington Post* would publish these papers—something her editors urged her to do, citing it was their duty to inform the public of the truth. The government felt publishing them was contrary to the "national welfare." Her lawyers, fearing retribution against the company, urged her not to publish them. Katharine stated in her memoir: "Frightened and tense, I took a big gulp and said, 'Go ahead, go ahead, go ahead. Let's go. Let's publish.'"[161]

Soon afterwards, *The Washington Post* reporters relentlessly covered the Watergate break-in, despite the threats made against the paper and Katharine herself. "I made a lot of speeches defending us during Watergate...I was trying to explain that we were reporting a story, that we weren't after the administration, and that it wasn't our intention to do them in. We were following the footsteps of the story..."[162] Revelations forced the resignation of President Nixon. On Friday, August 6, 1974, *The Washington Post* reported: "Richard Milhous Nixon announced last night that he will resign as the 37th President of the United States at noon today... After two years of bitter public debate over the Watergate scandals, President Nixon bowed to pressures from the public and leaders of his party to become the first President in American history to resign."[163]

Katharine was becoming known as one of the most powerful women in the country. She felt privileged to have such a unique connection to Washington's history, but knew it came with heavy duties. Her father had always taught her "that with privilege comes responsibilities..."[164]

When she spoke years later at C-SPAN on February 16, 1997, about her life, she summarized her role at *The Washington Post*: "...the *Post* has the power to inform people...I never see stories before they get in the papers. I have the power to pick an editor or publisher that will do the job well, and that is my general mode of thought. But after that, they have autonomy...I have more responsibility than power."[165]

She said, "[Today,] you have to influence events by giving people information by which they can make decisions..."[166]

At the age of 83, Katharine, who never wanted to stop work entirely despite retiring from The Washington Post Company nearly a decade earlier, decided to compile articles and memoirs by others into the book, *Katharine Graham's Washington*, where she stated: "I have been connected—either indirectly through my parents, or directly—with more than a third of all the presidents who have served the United States...I have 'known' sixteen of them. Even I was awed when faced with the facts."[167]

Katharine died at the age of 84 as the result of injuries sustained in a fall on her way to a bridge game. On July 17, 2001, *The New York Times* reported: "Katharine Graham, who transformed The Washington Post from a mediocre newspaper into an American institution and, in the process, transformed herself from a lonely widow into a publishing legend, died today..."[168]

Katharine now lies with her husband, Philip Graham, at Oak Hill Cemetery in Washington, D.C.

Questions for Discussion

- What philosophy of widowhood did Katharine adopt?

- She received a letter of consolation from Jackie Kennedy that she found helpful. What do you think that letter might have said?

- How did Katharine bridge the time/culture gaps that were articulated in the Women's Rights movement of her time?

- In what ways did Katharine show courage?

16. JULIA CHILD

Recipe for success

Author's note: When I saw the movie, Julie & Julia (2009), *starring Meryl Streep and Amy Adams, I was fascinated by Julia Child's love story and could relate to her years of struggle trying to get her cookbook written and published. The movie left me wondering about her life after her husband, Paul, died.*

Julia's cooking partner, acclaimed author and chef, Jacques Pépin, living not too far from me in Connecticut, was a guest on my local access TV show, and generously gave kitchen tips to those surviving spouses who had not been the family cook.[169]

When Julia McWilliams met her future husband, Paul Child, overseas during WWII in May 1944, neither was impressed with the other. Although both worked with the U.S. Office of Strategic Services (predecessor to the CIA), they had little else in common other than their desire to find a decent meal.

Julia was 6'2" and 31 years old, while Paul was a balding 42-year-old—and much too short for Julia's liking at 5'9". Paul was even less enthralled by Julia, who lacked his idea of sophistication. He was still recovering from the death of his love, Edith Kennedy—a woman he felt could never be equaled.

Julia and Paul were stationed in Ceylon (now Sri Lanka) and toured the area with friends. Although he wrote to his brother about Julia's long legs and "somewhat ragged, but pleasantly crazy sense of humor,"[170] she wasn't what he was looking for.

In January 1945, Paul flew to China to set up a war room. Although he and Julia had shared a few kisses, that appeared to be it for Paul – but not for Julia who was falling in love. When Julia was later transferred to China, they were eventually posted to the same region. Finally, it was food that brought them "together." The army fare was so awful; they often sought meals in restaurants together.

On August 6, an atomic bomb was dropped on Hiroshima. On August 14, the Japanese surrendered. The following day, Julia's 33rd birthday, Paul surrendered to Julia with the gift of his sonnet:

"How like the Autumn's warmth is Julia's face…
And how like the summer's heat is her embrace
Wherein at last she melts my frozen earth…"[171]

They were married at noon on September 1, 1946, in a civil ceremony in New Jersey. The reception was at Paul's brother's home across the river in Pennsylvania.

The Childs settled in Washington, D.C., where Paul worked mounting exhibits for the State Department. Having come from an affluent home in Pasadena, California, Julia had little idea how to cook—her family hired cooks. Paul loved fine food, and although they were limited to a government income, Julia was determined to prepare elegant meals. Equipped with the cookbook, *The Joy of Cooking*, and magazine recipes, she began to learn. Her first dinner featuring brains was barely edible.

In 1948, Paul was reassigned to the U.S. Information Service at the American Embassy in Paris, France. It was there Julia's passion to prepare French dishes was ignited. She never forgot their very first restaurant lunch of fish still sizzling in brown butter.

Julia couldn't have been happier—she was in love with her husband, and now Paris, for its "healthy pleasures of the flesh and spirit."[172]

And Paul loved his wife. He wrote to his brother in December 1948: "I love that woman." He listed some of the reasons why: "never once a harsh word, or bitterness, or a sense of disappointment."[173]

Julia enrolled at the famous Cordon Bleu cooking school. Told she had no real talent for cooking and even failing her final exam, she eventually earned her diploma. She and students Simone Beck and Louisette Bertholle formed their own cooking school and taught American women in Julia's kitchen.

Julia's cat, Minette, watched the lessons perched on her stool in hopes of getting samples. Unable to have children, Julia developed a passion for cats, beginning with Minette whom they adopted to control their kitchen mice.

Simone and Louisette asked Julia to collaborate on a French cookbook for Americans. Julia agreed providing she could also make it a teaching manual in addition to recipes using ingredients found in U.S. supermarkets (therefore, no ox blood). The women worked on the book for 10 years, producing more than 500 recipes with Paul taste-testing and photographing many of the dishes.

Paul resigned from the Foreign Service in 1960. Settling in Cambridge, Massachusetts, the postman finally delivered Julia's published book, *Mastering the Art of French Cooking*, on September 28, 1961.

Paul encouraged Julia to promote the book on the nearby Boston public television station, WGBH. He thought an audience would love Julia as much as he did. Convincing her to ignore the cameras and be herself, Julia's omelet demonstration was so successful she was asked to tape a series. *The French Chef* premiered in 1962, was syndicated across the U.S., won awards, and led to other TV appearances and books. Paul's support ranged from editing Julia's work to chopping onions and designing kitchens to accommodate her height.

Those happy years were interrupted when Paul began having chest pains. In 1974, he embarked on his long, slow decline after heart surgery and several strokes, which left him confused and incontinent. Julia still brought Paul wherever she could—TV rehearsals, meetings, receptions and dinner parties.

In 1989, Julia placed Paul in a nursing home—she could no longer care for him full-time. She visited him every day, sometimes several times a day, and called in between. He often didn't know who she was.

On May 12, 1994, after finishing taping a segment of *In Julia's Kitchen with Master Chefs*, with her Cambridge kitchen serving as the studio, the 82-year-old Julia visited Paul then went to dinner with friends and family. The restaurant received the call that signaled the end to their 48-year marriage—Paul had died. He was 92. Julia got the news in the middle of dessert and left immediately.

In August, family and friends gathered on rocky cliffs in Maine to scatter Paul's ashes to the sea. "So long, old boy," Julia said as the wind took his ashes. "Goodbye Sweetie," her nephew heard her say.[174]

Julia determined to stay busy. She still had the *In Julia's Kitchen* series to tape and several guest appearances on shows such as *Good Morning America*. Julia also appeared in shows with French chef and author Jacques Pépin, who, like Julia, taught classes at Boston University. When asked what Julia was like in her widow years, Jacques said she was glad for the work of their show. He had been friends with Paul and Julia since the 1960s. He fondly recalled the dinners he and his wife Gloria shared in their Cambridge home. "Julia and I would decide what to prepare and Paul would be in charge of the mixed drinks and photographing our meals."[175]

In 2001, at 89, Julia moved back to California where she enjoyed going for drives and to the movies with friends and family. By 2004, she became increasingly weak after knee surgery, which resulted in postoperative complications. She still loved, however, to reminisce about Paul. In late 2003, she began telling her story, *My Life in France*, to her grandnephew, freelance writer Alex Prud'homme. She wanted her story told, in part, to pay tribute to Paul. She loved editing Alex's written versions of her memories. She declared, "This book energizes me!"[176]

Julia introduced her memoir: "This is a book about some of the things I have loved most in my life: my husband, Paul Child; la belle France; and the many pleasures of cooking and eating...I was lucky to marry Paul...his encouragement saw me through discouraging moments. I would never have had a career without Paul Child."[177]

On August 12, 2004, Julia learned she had an infection requiring hospitalization. Realizing she would never really get better, she refused treatment, went to bed with a cat settled by her side, and never woke up. She died early morning of August 13, at the age of 91.

Julia's niece mingled Julia's ashes with her mother's and brought them to Paris. She sprinkled them under a tree, returning Julia to the city that, according to Julia, "marked a crucial period of transformation in which I found my true calling…"[178]

Julia's Cambridge kitchen is exhibited in the Smithsonian's National Museum of American History. Her life in France is told in the movie, *Julie & Julia* (2009), starring Meryl Streep and Amy Adams. The film is partially based on Julia's memoir, *My Life in France*, in which the last line of Julia's introduction reads: "I hope this book is as much fun for you to read as it was for us to put together—bon appetite!"[179]

Questions for Discussion

- Julia didn't have children. How did this influence her life?

- What was her passion after Paul's death?

- How did her life influence you?

---

17. CORETTA SCOTT KING

Marched on

Publisher's note: Martin Luther King, Jr. saw immediately in Coretta a woman who was strong enough to be his life partner. When they married, they really had no idea what their future held. I think that he would have been proud to see how bravely she carried on his life work. She raised their children to care about justice. Outside the home, her public speaking activities broke barriers for both blacks and women. This pastor's wife did more than bake pies!

It was 1968. Dr. Martin Luther King, Jr. was growing tired of marching, going to jail, and receiving constant death threats. Although there had been great victories in desegregation, the 39-year-old Baptist minister felt progress in the civil rights movement was slow. It had been over 12 years since Rosa Parks refused to give up her bus seat to a white man – the incident that launched Martin as a leader in the movement. It had been nearly five years since his famous "I Have a Dream" speech from the steps of the Lincoln Memorial in Washington in 1963, which included the line, "I have a dream that my four little children will one day live in a nation where they will not be judged by the color of their skin but by the content of their character."[180]

Despite Martin's weariness, he felt he should march the day after Easter 1968, on Monday, April 8, in support of the sanitation workers' grievances in Memphis, Tennessee. On Wednesday, April 3, he left his wife, Coretta, and their four children, ranging in age from five to 12, back home in Atlanta, Georgia. Despite the delay in his flight because of a bomb threat against him, he arrived in Memphis to give his speech that evening. Referring to the bomb threat, he said, "Like anybody, I would like to live a long life. Longevity has its place. But I'm not concerned about that now. I just want to do God's will. And He's allowed me to go up to the mountain. And I've looked over. And I've *seen* the promised land. I may not get there with you. But I want you to know tonight, that we, as a people, will get to the promised land!"[181]

The next day, Thursday, April 4, Coretta took their oldest child, Yolanda, dress shopping in preparation for Easter. Born less than three weeks before seamstress Rosa Parks refused to leave her seat in the front of the Negro section to accommodate a white man, Yolanda and her younger siblings grew up in the movement and knew its dangers. After returning home with her packages, Coretta received the call she had always feared. Jesse Jackson said, "Coretta, Doc just got shot."[182] He had been on the balcony of the Lorraine Motel when a sniper shot through Martin's right cheek at 6:01 p.m. He was unconscious.

Coretta immediately headed to the airport to catch a flight to Memphis. Before takeoff, however, she learned Martin had died. The 40-year-old widow decided to return home to be with her children that night. Coretta later wrote in her autobiography, *My Life with Martin Luther King, Jr.*, about that silent car ride home. "...It was strange, yet reassuring, that his death would come so close to the anniversary of the death of his Lord and Master...[Martin] would say that the moments of despair and doubt were the Good Fridays of life. But...even in the darkest moments, something happens and you hear the drums of Easter. As the clouds of despair begin to disperse, you realize that there is hope, and life, and light, and truth."[183] Then Coretta turned her thoughts to what she was going to tell the children.

Coretta flew to Memphis the following day, Good Friday, on a plane provided by Senator Robert Kennedy, to accompany Martin's body back to Atlanta. On Saturday, Coretta was asked if she would return to Memphis on Monday and march in her husband's place.

Yes, that is what Martin would have wanted her to do. So the day before this funeral on Tuesday, she took her three oldest children to Memphis and marched to City Hall. She said, "In the shock and sorrow of Martin's death the federal injunction against the march was either forgotten or rescinded; there was hardly a person in America who would have dared or even wanted to enforce it...There were dense crowds of people along the route who did not cheer or wave, but stood silent in Martin's memory."[184] The inspiration Coretta received from the supporters in Memphis "helped me to get through those first days and also the long days ahead."[185]

Born on April 27, 1927, Coretta Scott was raised in Marion, Alabama, where she picked cotton as a part-time job. After earning a B.A. in music and education, she studied concert singing at Boston's New England Conservatory of Music. While there in 1952, she met Martin Luther King, Jr. who was studying for his doctorate in systematic theology at Boston University. She was not impressed at first sight—he was too short.

But Martin was smitten from the moment he saw Coretta. He was from a prominent Atlanta family and told her on their first date that she filled the bill as a preacher's wife: "The four things that I look for in a wife are character, intelligence, personality, and beauty. And you have them all. I want to see you again. When can I?"[186]

Coretta did admire his intelligence and confidence. It took her six months from the time he proposed to say yes. Surrounded by 350 guests, she married Martin in her parents' garden in rural Alabama on June 18, 1953.

In September 1954, the couple moved to Montgomery, Alabama, where Martin served as pastor of the Dexter Avenue Baptist Church. Less than three weeks after the birth of Yolanda, on December 1, 1955, Rosa Parks refused to give up her seat in the Negro section of an overcrowded bus to a white man. Martin's time had come to take on a leadership role in civil rights. He had said, "Religion deals with both heaven and earth ....Any religion that professes to be concerned with the souls of men and is not concerned with the slums that doom them, the economic conditions that strangle them, and the social conditions that cripple them, is a dry-as-dust religion."[187]

Coretta supported Martin's decision to take on the cause and helped whenever she could between raising their growing family. She spoke before churches, colleges, and performed a series of Freedom Concerts which combined writings with music. In 1964, Coretta went to Norway with Martin where he received the Nobel Peace Prize.

Now Martin was gone, but injustice was not. Coretta said, "In the same way that I had given him all the support I could during his lifetime, I was even more determined to do so now that he was no longer with us. Because his task was not finished, I felt that I must rededicate myself to the completion of his work."[188]

Of course she had other concerns beyond the civil rights movement. She told Dr. Ralph Bryson, a friend from Dexter Avenue King Memorial Baptist Church, "I'll never get over Martin's death but I have to raise our children, and I'm going to do the very best that I can to do that."[189] She raised them to care about the cause.

At first, Coretta used Martin's words in her speeches and writings, but then she began speaking from her own heart and took on other causes. When she spoke for Martin at the Poor People's Campaign at the Lincoln Memorial on June 19, 1968, she not only shared his vision, but she asked women "to unite and form a solid block of women power to fight the three great evils of racism, poverty and war."[190]

Coretta traveled throughout the world speaking on human rights and consulted with many world leaders such as Nelson Mandela. In 1985, she and three of her children were arrested at the South African embassy in Washington, DC, for protesting against apartheid. Eventually she stood with Nelson Mandela in Johannesburg when he became South Africa's first democratically-elected president.

Coretta founded the Martin Luther King, Jr. Center for Nonviolent Social Change in Atlanta, which trains people from all over the world in Martin's ideals and methods. Her other major goal was to establish Martin's birthday as a national holiday. After years of lobbying, in January 1986, she oversaw the first legal holiday in honor of him.

Coretta died on January 30, 2006, at the age of 78. She and Martin now lie together in a memorial crypt at The King Center's Freedom Hall Complex. While Martin's half of the grave marker reads: "Free at last, Free at last, Thank God Almighty I'm Free at Last," Coretta's reads: "And now abide Faith, Hope, Love, These Three; but the greatest of these is love." 1 Corinthians 13:13.

End note: Now a 23-acre national historic park, The King Center attracts one million visitors a year. The grounds include Martin's birth home and the King Library and Archives, which, according to the Center's website, contains "the largest repository of primary source materials on Dr. Martin Luther King, Jr. and the American Civil Rights Movement in the world... The archives also include more than 200 oral history interviews with Dr. King's teachers, friends, family and civil rights associates." Learn more: www.thekingcenter.org.

Questions for Discussion

- Coretta supported Martin's work during her lifetime, and determined to continue with his life's work after his death. How did embracing the work that killed him influence her life and the life of others?

- How did his life and death influence how she raised their children? What other choices did she have?

- How is life after loss unique when the death was due to an inherently dangerous job or activity?

- How did she open the eyes of the public to create a better world for her children—and all of ours?

18. ABBY DAY SLOCOMB

A peek at a time capsule

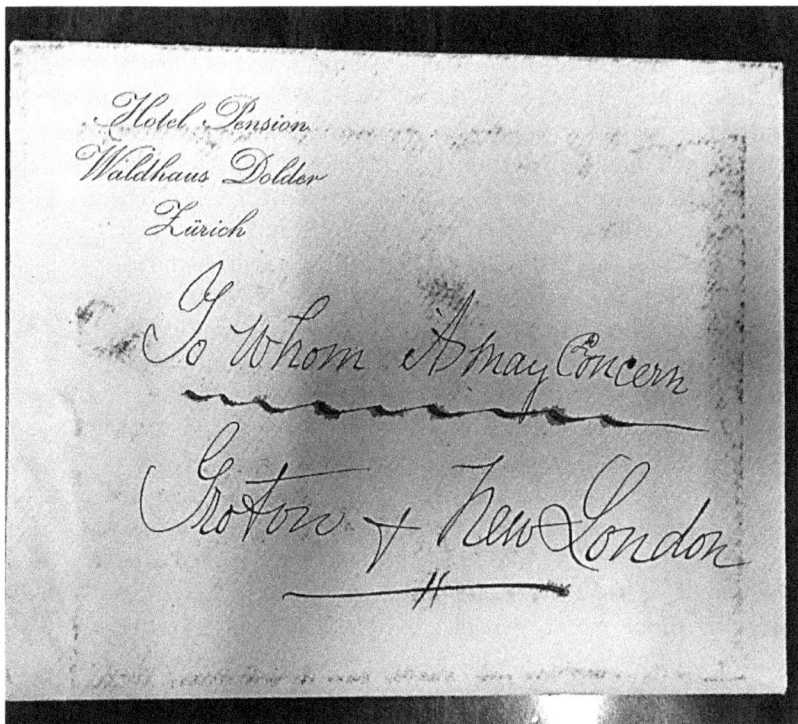

This letter was found when a 100-year-old time capsule was opened by the Anna Warner Bailey Chapter of the National Society of Daughters of the American Revolution (DAR) on September 6, 2014.

Author's note: In 1914, a time capsule was shipped to Groton, Connecticut, from Europe during WWI. I had the thrill of witnessing its opening a century later.

After sitting quietly hidden away at Fort Griswold Monument House Museum in Groton, Connecticut, for 100 years, the mysterious contents of a time capsule were revealed on September 6, 2014.

Widow Abigail (Abby) Day Slocomb, former Confederate Army nurse and first regent of the Anna Warner Bailey Chapter of the Daughters of the American Revolution (DAR), was 76 years old when she sent the soldered-shut tin case enclosed in a wooden box to her DAR chapter from her hotel in Zurich, Switzerland, during WWI in 1914. What kind of woman sends a time capsule—and why?

Born on October 5, 1838, and raised in New Orleans, Louisiana, Abby Day married Cuthbert Harrison Slocomb of New Orleans and served as a nurse for the Confederate Army behind enemy (Union) lines while her husband served as an officer. One day, Abby found her husband among her patients after he was badly wounded carrying dispatches to General Robert E. Lee. Abby took Cuthbert home to recuperate.

Abby's husband died less than a decade after the Civil War's end in 1873, leaving her a widow at the age of 35. In 1888, Abby, well familiar with Connecticut where her family was from, moved to Monument Street in Groton. Her home was next to Fort Griswold, the site of the Battle of Groton Heights, which overlooked New London across the Thames River. Abby named her home "Daisy Crest Over Groton."[191]

As the great-granddaughter of Abigail Dolbeare and Capt. Elisha Hinman, a New London privateer during the American Revolution; and granddaughter of mariner Capt. James Day, "who, during the War of 1812, deliberately wrecked his vessel off Point Judith to prevent its capture by the British,"[192] Abby was asked by the Daughters of the American Revolution (founded 1890) to be the first regent of the Anna Warner Bailey Chapter (organized 1893).

Initially, Abby declined the regent position, but later accepted. She wrote in her logbook, "I had a patriotic obligation and when I was asked again, I picked it up."[193] She wanted the Chapter named after her great-grandmother, Abigail Dolbeare Hinman, for her brave—yet failed—attempt to shoot traitor Benedict Arnold while he commanded British, Hessian, and Loyalist troops to burn New London and attack his former countrymen at Fort Griswold, located right beside her present home.

Despite Abby's desire to see her ancestor Abigail Dolbeare Hinman honored, Chapter members voted instead to name their chapter in memory of Anna Warner Bailey, known as "Mother Bailey," a childless woman who tended the wounded after the massacre at Fort Griswold and was later honored by U.S. presidents for removing her flannel petticoat in the middle of the street when soldiers needed wadding for their muskets against a British attack anticipated during the War of 1812.[194]

Although Abby did not win the fight to name the chapter after her ancestor, under Abby's determined guidance and dedication to her "patriotic obligation," her chapter was responsible for the design of the Connecticut State flag, based on the 1639 Connecticut seal, and organization of the Monument House Museum at Fort Griswold, which displays artifacts from the September 6, 1781, massacre including Colonel William Ledyard's sword. (When Col. Ledyard surrendered the fort to the British, the fight went from a battle to a massacre. It was said that Ledyard was rammed through with his own sword after stepping forward with it pointing toward himself in the act of surrender. When Ledyard's nephew and others moved to avenge their commander's death, all were stabbed repeatedly by bayonet—one as many as 30 times. Colonists hiding at the fort were tracked down and bayoneted to death. In the meantime, Benedict Arnold ordered New London burned.)

In 1906, when Abby Day Slocomb's married daughter living in Europe became ill, Abby left her Groton home to care for her. Abby did not, however, stop performing her patriotic duty toward her homeland. When what was to become known as the Great War broke out, she sent a message to future members of her DAR chapter—none of whom had been born yet. Abby compiled items into a tin box, had it soldered shut, placed it inside a wooden box, then shipped it to her DAR chapter in Groton with the instructions: "To be opened, year 2014."[195] A letter accompanied it from a U.S. Special Commissioner dated March 1, 1915, which stated that the "package is to be passed at the port of arrival without examination of its contents, and WITHOUT DESTRUCTION OF THE INNER METAL CASE."[196]

Abby did not live long enough to see the war's end, which was one of the bloodiest wars of all time. She died three years after sending the time capsule at the age of 79 on December 6, 1917. She is buried at Enzenbuhl, Zurich, Switzerland. The war ended on November 11, 1918, on what was known as Armistice Day, later changed to Veteran's Day.

Fast forward 100 years: the day scheduled to open the time capsule was finally approaching. The time capsule was removed from the safe at the Fort Griswold Monument House Museum and put on display.

Members of the Daughters of the American Revolution and their invited guests arrived for the time capsule opening on September 6, 2014, the 233rd anniversary of traitor Benedict Arnold's burning of New London and massacre at Fort Griswold.

The expectant audience watched Joe de la Cruz of Hillery Company, a metal-fabrication manufacturer, cut the time capsule open while the portrait of Abby Day Slocomb looked on. Beyond the wall behind the time capsule was Fort Griswold where one can still imagine the carnage that took place 233 years earlier. A plaque marks the spot where Col. Ledyard was rammed through with his own sword and fort remains include a tunnel-like passageway.

When the final cut was made to the time capsule, Janet F. Purinton, the regent of the Anna Warner Bailey Chapter (a descendant of Captain

Hubbard Burrows, one of the first killed in the Battle of Groton Heights), withdrew an envelope placed on top of the box's contents.

Janet read aloud Abby's envelope addressed: "To Whom It May Concern." After commenting, "We are the ones it concerns," Janet carefully opened the envelope.

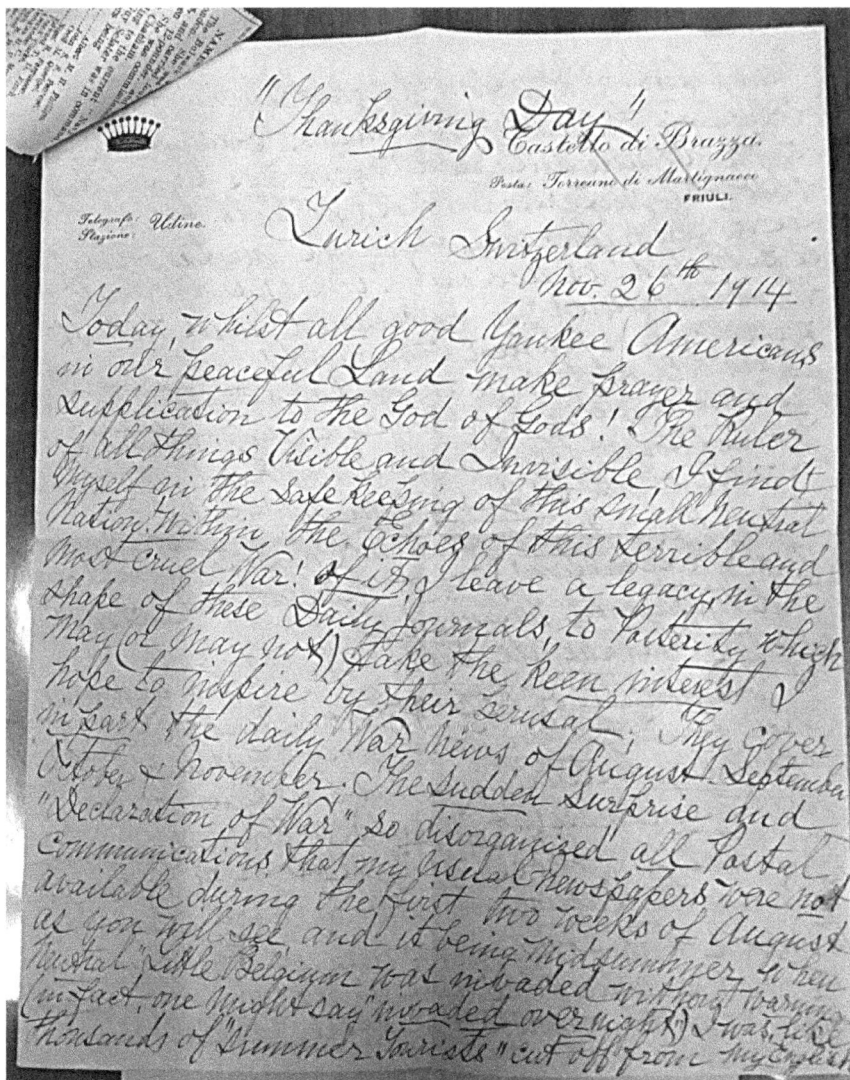

Pulling out the handwritten letter from Abby, Janet began to read aloud the message Abby felt compelled to write a century earlier during

WWI. The group sat motionless as they absorbed Abby's message from beyond the grave:

"Thanksgiving Day"
Zurich Switzerland   Nov 26th 1914

Today, whilst all good Yankee Americans in our Peaceful Land make prayer and supplication to the God of Gods! The Ruler of all things Visible and Invisible, I find myself in the Safe Keeping of this small neutral Nation! Within the Echoes of this terrible and most cruel War! Of it, I leave a legacy, in the shape of these Daily Journals, to Posterity which May or (May not) take the keen interest I hope to inspire by their perusal; They cover in part the daily War News of August, September, October, & November.   The Sudden Surprise and "Declaration of War" so disorganized all Postal communications, that my usual newspapers were not available during the first two weeks of august as you will see, and it being mid-summer when Neutral "little Belgium" was invaded without warning (in fact, one might say "invaded overnight") I was like thousands of "Summer Tourists" cut off from my English Newspapers; I then found enlightenment and solace in the admirable Milan Daily issue of the "Corrier della Sera" which has proved itself absolutely impartial in its methods; You will see its Telegraphic News from all quarters of Europe is published as received! One Report following the other "censored" or "uncensored" and without prejudiced or political comment! We are told that in the early days of the War the "Corrier della Sera" was eagerly watched & waited for at the Kaiser's army Headquarters because of its "Editorial Column"! which is assuredly (under the caption "La Situazione" or Eng "The Situation") most unprejudiced! clear! and intelligently balanced! In the "Almanac de Gotha" The Kaiser is entered as William II of Hohenzollern-King & Emperor! etc. etc but I am wondering what descriptive appellation posterity will have affixed to this most hated man (at present) in the entire civilized World! I hope he will go down in History as "William the Destroyer"! "Bloody Mary"- Queen of England was so named because of the few hundred sacrifices she made in her religious fanaticism. Then what can describe and atone for this Kaiser's millions of human beings sacrificed to his vanity! For the homes wiped off the Earth and the universal destruction carried out at his command & in which he seems to absolutely revel! Is he a mad- man! thirsting for blood? I have lived, served & suffered through both the five years of Civil War & the Spanish American War! and now, in my old age I seek in vain for an absolutely unprejudiced & true History of those trying days! Circumstances now prevent me continuing this collection of newspapers as I am leaving this peaceful "Haven of Rest" for a region unprovided with an American Consulate to seal up *these chronicles! which therefore must end on the 29ᵗʰ of this month, <u>long before</u> this unparalled <u>sanguinary</u> struggle will cease its continuous <u>night</u> and <u>day</u> Slaughter! I <u>pray</u> even these few contemporary Sheets of "Reports" may inspire someone to make a sincere & dispassionate <u>investigation</u> of the Sad <u>true</u> Story of this <u>terrific</u> episode in Human History! I confide them to the care of The Anna Warner Bailey Chapter of Groton and Stonington Daughters of the American Revolution! to be by then, in case their Chapter should be broken up - at any future time – turned over to the "New London Historical Society." One Hundred Years hence you will (as now) doubtless find intelligent Italians <u>in your</u> neighborhood capable & willing to translate the majority of these pages for you.*

Abby Day Slocomb

Organizer and Hon. Regent of the AWB Chapter <u>D.A.R.</u>

<u>P.S.</u> I am wondering if <u>women</u> <u>in</u> <u>2014</u> will still be adding Post -Scripts to their letters! Mine is to apologize for my Son-in-Laws private letter papers! I find it in my port-folio and owing to the War <u>no</u> <u>large</u> sheets of durable writing paper can <u>be</u> <u>had</u> in <u>this</u> <u>Hotel</u>. A. D. S.[197]

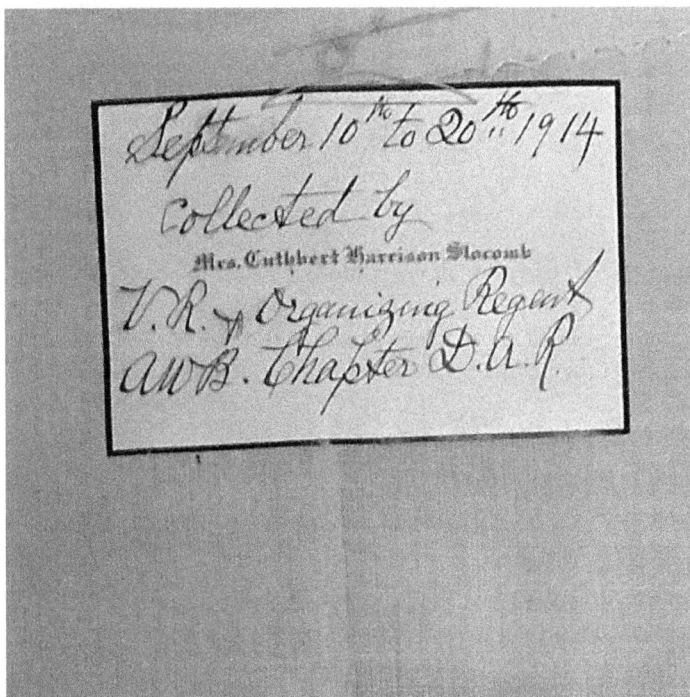

Next, Janet opened one of the several hand-sewn linen packets pulled from the time capsule. It included news clippings.

favor of the Sultan, who has always appeared to them to be a parvenu?

The "Idea Nazionale" says that inaction on the part of Italy with the new phase of the war before her would be simply an absurd blindness.

The "Giornale d'Italia" arrives at an almost similar conclusion. "Let us keep cool," it says. "Let us not ignore the fact that the cataclysm of war which is extending will inevitably create a new system which will have its repercussion in Italy. It is more than ever important that our neutrality should be vigilant and above all strongly armed."—Temps.

IS THE KAISER MAD?

PETROGRAD, Thursday. — The Russian papers are more and more inclined to take the view that Emperor William is insane. They cite to-day his proclamation to the Poles at Czenstochow, in which he referred to a miraculous ringing of the bells at the Sviatogorosky monastery and declared that it denoted his decision to make war on Russia, restore the sacred possessions of Poland and unite Poland to Germany, the most cultured country. The Kaiser added : "I had a wondrous dream. The Virgin appeared to me and entrusted me with the rescue of her sacred habitation. She gazed at me tearfully, and I went forth to execute her holy will."

The Kaiser called on the Poles to meet the German troops as their brothers and saviors. Those who were with him, he said, would be amply rewarded, while those who were against him would perish. He concluded with these words: "With me are God and the Holy Virgin, who have drawn the German sword in aid of Poland."—Reuter.

Discouraged that she never found an unprejudiced account of the American Civil War and Spanish American War, Abby hoped that the 1914 news clippings—ones of note she marked in red—would inspire someone in 2014 to investigate "the sad true story of this terrific episode in Human History!"

Clipping headlines in the first packet include:

- IS THE KAISER MAD?[198]
- "NOT A GENTLEMAN." KING EDWARD'S OPINION OF THE KAISER
- "ANNIHILATE THE ENGLISH." ANOTHER ROYAL GERMAN ORDER
- OVER 100 SHOTS. EYE-WITNESSES' STIRRING NARRATIVES
- GERMAN'S DIARY SHOWS KAISER WAS BENT ON WAR
- ITALY STOPS EXPORTS

Of the rest of the packets yet to be opened, Janet said, "We do indeed have many hours of history which we're anxious to share. Historic Preservation Chairman Louisa Watrous will be opening, cataloguing and storing all the information in archival boxes, which will take a bit of time."

As of this writing, cataloging of the time capsule is still in process, with data recording in PastPerfect (collection management software for museums) in collaboration with the State of Connecticut. The Anna Warner Bailey Chapter now has a volunteer to help open the packets, which are sewn tightly shut. Only time will tell what new and unbiased truths they will reveal.

"I pray even these few contemporary Sheets of 'Reports' may inspire someone to make a sincere & dispassionate investigation of the Sad true Story of this terrific episode in Human History..." Abby Day Slocomb.

Publisher's Note: Most of the stories in this book are placed chronologically, according to the date of death. So this chapter may seem out of place to an observant reader. We decided to place it last, because we feel that the story has not yet ended. We believe that more information will be forthcoming, so we'll just say... To be continued!

Author's Note: Undoubtedly, one cause of Abby Day Slocomb's passion toward her patriotic duty was her knowing the role her great-grandmother, Abigail Dolbeare Hinman, played during the American Revolution. When her uncle, Thomas Davis Day, commissioned artist Daniel Huntington to paint Abigail Dolbeare Hinman standing beside a window with her rifle, while Benedict Arnold sat on horseback watching New London burn, Abby Day Slocomb served as the model when she was approximately 16. Abby wore the ball gown believed to belong to her great-grandmother Abigail. According to author Nancy Rash, Thomas Day told his sisters "that the works of art would provide 'an incentive to all our children to keep inviolate the respectability of the family.'"[199] (The painting can be seen at the Lyman Allyn Art Museum in New London, Connecticut.)[200]

To learn more about the time capsule or the Anna Warner Bailey Chapter of the National Society of Daughters of the American Revolution, visit: http://annawarnerbaileydar.org. The mission of the National Society Daughters of the American Revolution is to perpetuate the memory and the spirit of the men and women who achieved American Independence; to promote the development of an enlightened public opinion, and to foster patriotic citizenship.

To learn more about the Fort Griswold Battlefield State Park and Monument House Museum, visit: www.fortgriswold.org/the-monument-and-museum.

I wrote an account of the Battle at Groton Heights and "Mother Bailey" in my travel memoir, *Mystic Seafarer's Trail.*

Questions for Discussion

- If you were to put together a time capsule for your descendants to open in a 100 years, what would you put in it?

- Abby was passionate about the world having an unbiased account of WWI because she never found one of the Civil War or Spanish American War. What about your life experiences do you want clearly understood and remembered?

ABOUT AUTHOR LISA SAUNDERS

Lisa Saunders with a picture of her daughter, Elizabeth (1989-2006), next to Connecticut Governor Dan Malloy at the ceremonial bill signing for Public Act 15-10: An Act Concerning Cytomegalovirus at the Office of the Governor in Hartford on July 28, 2015.

Lisa Saunders is an award-winning writer and TV talk show host living in Mystic, Connecticut, with her husband, Jim, and hound, Doolittle. A graduate of Cornell University, she is the author of several books and publisher of a Mystic newsletter. She works as a part-time history interpreter at Mystic Seaport, instructor at New London Adult & Continuing Education on publishing and publicity, and writes website content for clients. Lisa is a member of the Daughters of the American Revolution (Anna Warner Bailey Chapter) and is the parent representative of the Congenital Cytomegalovirus Foundation. She and her husband serve as cadet sponsors for the U.S. Coast Guard Academy.

Lisa first became interested in American history as a young woman when the family genealogist, David Sisson, uncovered interesting ancestry. She descends from *Mayflower* passenger, Richard Warren, from Benjamin Church, considered to be the father of the U.S. Army Rangers, and from Captain Henry Gale, a Revolutionary War veteran found guilty of high treason and sentenced to be hanged for his leadership role in Shays' Rebellion. Lisa figured if her ancestors could impact history, so could she.

Lisa said, "I have struggled for years, since the birth of my severely disabled daughter Elizabeth in 1989, to ensure that women of child-bearing age know how to protect their unborn children from the leading viral cause of birth defects, congenital cytomegalovirus (CMV). According to the Centers for Disease Control and Prevention (CDC), every hour a child in the U.S. is born disabled by congenital CMV, yet most pregnant women have never heard of it or their need to be careful around the bodily fluids of toddlers who are often shedding the virus."

Finally, in 2015, Lisa succeeded—with the help of parents and the medical community—in getting Connecticut to become one of the few states in the U.S. to enact a law aimed at fighting this devastating disease. Lisa's work, however, is not done. "My hope is to persevere until all doctors make it a standard practice of care to educate women of childbearing age on congenital CMV prevention, or, until an effective vaccine is made available."

Books by Lisa Saunders

- > *After the Loss of a Spouse, Henry VIII to Julia Child.* Examines the bittersweet human condition of love and loss though the lens of history. By learning how these famous—and infamous— people managed their lives after the loss of a spouse, we come to realize the potential that exists in all of us.
- > *Anything But a Dog! The perfect pet for a girl with congenital CMV (cytomegalovirus).* Lisa's memoir about raising her daughters—one severely disabled—alongside their dysfunctional pets.
- > *Ever True: A Union Private and His Wife.* Civil War love letters.
- > *Images of Modern America: Mystic.* Co-authored with Kent and Meredith Fuller.
- > *Lisa's Guide for Writers* includes how to get published—even if you're not thin and famous!
- > *Mystic Seafarer's Trail: Secrets behind the 7 Wonders, Titanic's Shoes, Captain Sisson's Gold, and Amelia Earhart's Wedding.* A travel memoir.
- > *Once Upon a Placemat: A Table Setting Tale.* Booklet includes a table setting fairytale explaining why Mr. Knife is afraid the dish will run away with the spoon, images for coloring, plus how to prevent the leading viral cause of birth defects by reminding families not to share cups and utensils with each other without washing them first.
- > *Ride a Horse Not an Elevator.* A children's novel.
- > *Shays' Rebellion: The Hanging of Henry Gale.* Short booklet.
- > *Surviving Loss: The Woodcutter's Tale.* Lisa's father wrote a fairytale after her daughter died. The booklet includes comments by Lisa and Julie Russell, MSW, LCSW, to help individuals understand the grieving process so they can return to a life with purpose and meaning.

To schedule Lisa Saunders as a speaker or to order her books, contact her directly at LisaSaunders42@gmail.com or visit AuthorLisaSaunders.com.

ABOUT ACT II PUBLICATIONS, LLC

Act II Publications, LLC, was founded by Dr. Joanne Z. Moore in 2013 to support people as they rebuild their lives after loss.

Among its publications are:

- Guidebook: *After the Loss of a Spouse: What's Next?* by Dr. Joanne Z Moore. Available at www.Amazon.com

- Biographies: *After the Loss of a Spouse, From Henry VIII to Julia Child* by Lisa Saunders. Available on Amazon, PathfinderMag.com, AuthorLisaSaunders.com

- E-Magazine: *Pathfinder: A Companion Guide for the Widow/er's Journey.* See www.PathfinderMag.com

- Free newsletter: Receive monthly news, articles, retreats, and recipes by subscribing at www.PathfinderMag.com

Looking for speakers, books, retreats, magazines? Contact:

Dr. Joanne Z. Moore
PO Box 752, East Lyme CT, 06333.
JMoore@widowedpathfinder.com
860-448-5149
www.PathfinderMag.com
www.facebook.com/pathfindermagazine

Our next book in the series:
After the Loss of a Spouse: A New Romance by Joanne Z Moore

BIBLIOGRAPHY and END NOTES

AAUW Coretta Scott King Fellows: Scholars and Women of Action. (n.d.).
Retrieved April 1, 2016, from American Association of University
Women: http://www.aauw.org/2012/02/29/coretta-scott-king-
fellows/

Abigail Hannah "Abby" Day Slocomb. (n.d.). Retrieved October 11, 2014,
from Find a Grave: http://www.findagrave.com/cgi-
bin/fg.cgi?page=gr&GRid=80446277

About Mrs. King. (n.d.). Retrieved November 9, 2015, from The King
Center: http://www.thekingcenter.org/about-mrs-king

About Norman Rockwell. (n.d.). Retrieved April 16, 2016, from Norman
Rockwell Museum: http://www.nrm.org/about-2/about-norman-
rockwell/

Adler, J. . (2015, January). *Will the Search for Amelia Earhart Ever End?* .
Retrieved from Smithsonian.com:
http://www.smithsonianmag.com/history/will-search-for-amelia-
earhart-ever-end-180953646/?page=1&no-ist

AMELIA EARHART BIOGRAPHICAL SKETCH. (n.d.). Retrieved
2012, from Purdue University George Palmer Collections of
Amelia Earhart Papers :
http://www.lib.purdue.edu/spcol/aearhart/biography.php

Anderson, J. R. (2012, September 26). Lawyer. (L. Saunders, Interviewer)

Anderson, J. R. (November 17, 2010). *Amelia Earhart in Noank.* Retrieved
from Noank Historical Society, Inc., Research Files: Paper given to
Ariston Club, New London, and Noank Historical Society.

Anderson, M. (2012, August). Curator, Noank Historical Society. (L.
Saunders, Interviewer) Noank, Connecticut. Retrieved from
http://www.noankhistoricalsociety.org/

Anna Warner Bailey Chapter, Daughters of American Revolution. (n.d.).
Sec. Record Book April 29, 1913. *Page 282, 02-AWB.042.*

*Anna Warner Bailey Chapter, National Society of the Daughters of the American
Revolution.* (n.d.). Retrieved April 16, 2016, from
http://annawarnerbaileydar.org/index.html

Another Look at Hetty Green, The Witch of Wall Street. (n.d.). Retrieved July 21,
2014, from New England Historical Society:
http://www.newenglandhistoricalsociety.com/another-look-hetty-
green-witch-wall-street/

Anyone Buried in Capitol. (n.d.). Retrieved April 16, 2016, from Architect of
the Capitol: http://www.aoc.gov/capitol-hill/anyone-buried-
capitol

Applebome, P. (2006, January 31). *Coretta Scott King, 78, Widow of Dr. Martin Luther King Jr., Dies*. Retrieved from New York Times: http://www.nytimes.com/2006/01/31/national/31cnd-coretta.html?_r=0

Archaeological Preserve, East Haddam, Connecticut, primary author: Richard G. Schaefer, Phd. (2004). *His Belove Aunt Polly*. Westport, Connecticut: Historical Perspectives, Inc.

Baker, E. (Fall 2006). Benedict Arnold Turns and Burns New London. *HOG RIVER JOURNAL, renamed CONNECTICUT EXPLORED*. Retrieved October 18, 2014, from New London County Historical Society: http://nlhistory.org/?p=452

Barey, Patricia; Burson, Therese. (2012). *Julia's Cats: Julia Child's Life in the Company of Cats*. New York: Abrams Image.

Baughman, J.P. (1972). *The Mallorys of Mystic: Six Generations in American Maritime Enterprise*. Middletown, Connecticut: Wesleyan University Press.

BERGER, M. (2001, July 17). *Katharine Graham, Former Publisher of Washington Post, Dies at 84*. Retrieved from New York Times: http://www.nytimes.com/2001/07/17/obituaries/17CND-GRAHAM.html?pagewanted=print

Biography of Amelia Earhart. (n.d.). Retrieved September 16, 2012, from Amelia Earhart Birthplace Museum: http://www.ameliaearhartmuseum.org/AmeliaEarhart/AEBiography.htm

Biography.com Editors . (2016, March 8). *Katharine Graham Biography* . Retrieved from The Biography.com website : http://www.biography.com/people/katharine-graham-9317709

Biography.com Editors. (2016, April 16). *Norman Rockwell Biography*. Retrieved from The Biography.com website: www.biography.com/people/norman-rockwell-37249

Biography.com Editors. (n.d.). *Corette Scott King*. Retrieved November 9, 2015, from Biography.com: http://www.biography.com/people/coretta-scott-king-9542067

Biography.com Editors. (n.d.). *George Burns Biography*. Retrieved April 16, 2016, from The Biography.com website: Biography.com: http://www.biography.com/people/george-burns-9232145

Biography.com Editors. (n.d.). *Henry VIII Biography*. Retrieved April 16, 2016, from The Biography.com website: http://www.biography.com/people/henry-viii-9335322#Katherine-of-aragon-and-princess-mary

Biography.com Editors. (n.d.). *Julia Child Biography*. Retrieved April 16, 2016, from The Biography.com website: http://www.biography.com/people/julia-child-9246767

Biography.com Editors. (n.d.). *Mark Twain Biography*. (A. T. Networks, Producer) Retrieved 20 November, 2015, from The Biography.com website.

Biography.com Editors. (n.d.). *Martha Washington Biography*. Retrieved April 16, 2016, from The Biography.com website: http://www.biography.com/people/martha-washington-9524817

Biography.com Editors. (n.d.). *Mary Todd Lincoln Biography*. Retrieved April 16, 2016, from The Biography.com website : http://www.biography.com/people/mary-todd-lincoln-248868

Biography.com Editors. (n.d.). *Milton Hershey Biography*. Retrieved April 16, 2016, from The Biography.com website: http://www.biography.com/people/milton-hershey-9337133#synopsis&awesm=~oDcpmoPjWvuSc0

Black, A. (2009). *The White House*. Retrieved 2014, from Martha Washington: http://www.whitehouse.gov/about/first-ladies/marthawashington

Borgens, A. (2014, April 8). State Marine Archeologist, Texas Historical Commission. (L. Saunders, Interviewer)

Borgens, A. (Spring 2013). Descent into Darkness: Texas Historical Commission Assists with Two Historic Shipwreck Investigations in Low-Visibility Waters. *Texas Historical Commission*.

Brown, S. (2014, June 20). Last of Her Kind, Waleship Charles W. Morgan Has Strong Ties to the Vineyard. *Vineyard Gazette*.

Burns, G. (1988). *Gracie: A Love Story*. New York: G.P. Putnam's Sons.

Burns, K. (Director). (2001). *Mark Twain* [Motion Picture].

Carol Berkin, Revolutionary Mothers: Women in the Struggle for America's Independence. (n.d.). Retrieved October 11, 2014, from Courses: Texas Tech University: http://courses.ttu.edu/instoll/HIST2300/2006/study_questions_Berkin.htm

Certificate of Marriage. (1931, February 7). Retrieved from Pres. Edward Elliot's Residence 1930-1940: http://earchives.lib.purdue.edu/cdm4/document.php?CISOROOT=/earhart&CISOPTR=3003&REC=1

Charles C. Sisson Papers (Coll. 114). (n.d.). Retrieved September 16, 2012, from Mystic Seaport: Museum of America and the Sea, Manuscript Collection Registers: http://library.mysticseaport.org/manuscripts/coll/coll114.cfm#restrictlink

Chef Jacques Pépin: Cooking for Widow/ers, Dr. Joanne Z. Moore, Pathfinder, Lisa Saunders Show. (2015, August 13). (L. Saunders, Producer, & Southeastern Connecticut Television Studios) Retrieved from YouTube: https://www.youtube.com/watch?v=WB891yRO90A

Child, Julia with Prud'homme, Alex. (2006). *My Life in France*. New York: Anchor Books, A Division of Random House, Inc.

City of Waco Disaster. (1875, November 11). *The Galveston Daily News*.

Claridge, L. (2001). *Norman Rockwell: a life*. New York: Random House.

Cleary, M. (1991). *Grandma Moses*. New York: Cresent Books.

Coin for Charon. (2016, April 16). Retrieved from Cyclopaedia.net: http://www.cyclopaedia.info/wiki/Coin-for-Charon

Connecticut (U.S.). (n.d.). Retrieved October 11, 2014, from Connecticut Flag: http://www.crwflags.com/fotw/flags/us-ct.html

Connecticut State Department of Health. (1930, November 8). Marriage License. Groton, Connecticut.

Conradt, S. (n.d.). *How the Titanic Almost Sank Hershey*. Retrieved April 14, 2016, from Mental Floss: http://mentalfloss.com/article/28766/how-titanic-almost-sank-hershey

CURLAND, R. (2008, August 27). Historically Speaking: Stonington-born woman helped create flag. *Norwich Bulletin*. Retrieved October 11, 2014, from http://www.norwichbulletin.com/x633546852/Historically-Speaking-Stonington-born-woman-helped-create-flag

Descendants of Richard (1608-1684) and Mary (d. 1692) SISSON of Rhode Island, Eight Generation. (n.d.). Retrieved September 19, 2012, from Rootsweb: http://homepages.rootsweb.ancestry.com/~dasisson/richard/aqwg114.htm#32218

Descendants of Richard (1608-1684) and Mary (d. 1692) SISSON of Rhode Island, Ninth Generation. (n.d.). Retrieved September 19, 2012, from Rootsweb: http://homepages.rootsweb.ancestry.com/~dasisson/richard/aqwg172.htm#32225

Dorothy Putnam. (n.d.). Retrieved from St. Lucie Historical Society, Inc.: http://martincountydemocr.easycgi.com/stlucie/dorothyputnam.htm

Earhart, A. (1931, February 7). *Letter, 1931 Feb. 7, Noank, Conn., to GPP (draft)*. Retrieved from Pres. Edward Elliot's Residence 1930-1940: http://earchives.lib.purdue.edu/cdm4/document.php?CISOROOT=/earhart&CISOPTR=2999&REC=16

Earhart, A. (1931, Feb. 7). *Letter, Noank, Conn., to GPP*. Retrieved April 16, 2016, from Purdue University Libraries: http://e-archives.lib.purdue.edu/cdm/singleitem/collection/earhart/id/298/rec/4

Ephron, N. (Director). (2009). *Julie & Julia* [Motion Picture].

Erickson, C. . (1980). *Great Harry*. New York: St. Martin's Griffin.

Exhibitions. (n.d.). Retrieved October 11, 2014, from Lyman Allyn Art Museum: http://www.lymanallyn.org/exhibitions/

Exhibitions and Collections. (n.d.). Retrieved from Lyman Allyn Art Museum: http://www.lymanallyn.org/?s=Daniel+Huntington+

Explore Lincoln: Learn the Story. (2016, April 16). Retrieved from Ford's Theatre: http://www.fordstheatre.org/index.php?q=home/explore-lincoln/learn-story

First Lady Biography: Martha Washington. (n.d.). Retrieved April 16, 2016, from National First Ladies Library: http://www.firstladies.org/biographies/firstladies.aspx?biography=1

Fitch, Noel Riley. (1977). *Appetite for Life: The Biography of Julia Child*. New York : Doubleday.

Fleischner, J. . (2003). *Mrs. Lincoln and Mrs. Keckly*. New York: Random House, Inc.

Freidel, Frank and Sidey, Hugh. (2006). *George Washington*. Retrieved 2014, from The White House: http://www.whitehouse.gov/about/presidents/georgewashington

Gaffney, D. (2008, January 7). *Mark Twain's "Aquarium"*. Retrieved from Antique Roadshow: http://www.pbs.org/wgbh/roadshow/fts/baltimore_200701A20.html

Gearin, J. (Winter 2005, Vol. 37, No. 4). *Movie vs. Reality:The Real Story of the von Trapp Family*. Retrieved from National Archives: http://www.archives.gov/publications/prologue/2005/winter/von-trapps.html

George Palmer Putnam. (n.d.). Retrieved 2015, from Find a Grave: http://www.findagrave.com/cgi-bin/fg.cgi?page=gr&GRid=8279482

GILLETTE AT LAST CAPITULATES TO AN INTERVIEWER. (1914, November 1). *The New York Times*. Retrieved 2014

Gillette Castle State Park. (n.d.). Retrieved April 16, 2016, from Department of Energy and Environmental Protection: http://www.ct.gov/deep/cwp/view.asp?a=2716&q=325204&deepNav_GID=1650

Gottfriend, M. (1996). *George Burns: The Hundred Yard Dash*. Simon & Schuster.

Graham, K. (1997). *Personal History*. New York: Alfred A. Knopf, Inc.

Graham, K. (1999). Katharine Graham. In B. Lamb, *BOOKNOTES: Life Stories* (p. 238). New York: Three Rivers Press, Crown Publishing Group, National Cable Satellite Corporation.

Graham, K. (2002). *Katharine Graham's Washington.* New York: Alfred A. Knopf.

Grandma Moses is Dead at 101: Primitive Artist 'Just wore out'. (1961, Dec 14). *The New York Times: ProQuest Historical Newspapers,* p. 1.

Green, Hetty. (1990). *Library of North American Biographies, Volume 3: Entrepreneurs ' Inventors.* The H.W. Wilson Company: Philip Lief.

Groton's Tercentennial Committee. (c. 2005). Designer of Our State Flag. *Mystic River Press.*

Hall, A. (2005, April). Ship Went Down in 1875 Fire: City of Waco Located in Galveston Bay. *Current Archeology in Texas.* Texas: Texas Historical Commission.

Hall, A. (2014, April 4). researcher and author from Galveston, Texas. (L. Saunders, Interviewer)

Hamilton, T. L. (2014, May 13, May 13). Archivist, Hershey Community Archives . (L. Saunders, Interviewer)

Hanna, D. (2012, September 14). Collections Manager, Mystic River Historical Society. (L. Saunders, Interviewer)

Henrietta (Hetty) Howland Robinson Green (1834-1916) – "The Witch of Wall Street". (n.d.). Retrieved July 15, 2014, from New Bedford Whaling Musueum : http://www.whalingmuseum.org/learn/hetty-green

Henry VIII (2008). [Motion Picture].

Henry VIII. (2016, April 1). Retrieved from The Official Website of the British Monarchy: http://www.royal.gov.uk/HistoryoftheMonarchy/KingsandQueensofEngland/TheTudors/HenryVIII.aspx

Hershey, Catherine Sweeney; 1871-1915 . (n.d.). Retrieved April 15, 2016, from Hershey Community Archives: http://www.hersheyarchives.org/essay/details.aspx?EssayId=11&Rurl=%2fresources%2fsearch-results.aspx%3fType%3dBrowseEssay

HETTY GREEN DIES, WORTH $100,000,000: Passes Away at Son's Home After Several Paralytic Strokes, Aged 82. HOPED TO LIVE TO BE 85 Invested Heavily in Bonds and Mortgages in Recent Years. (1916, July 4). *The New York Times.*

HETTY GREEN TALKS CASH AND POLITICS: Says Men Who Know Tell Her Roosevelt Will Be Nominated Again. REJECTED VANDERBILT GEMS Not Good Security for a Loan -- She Helped the New York Central and Others at 6 Per Cent. HETTY GREEN TALKS CASH AND POLITICS. (1908, February 15). *The New York Times.*

Hetty Green's Son and Heir Trained by Her: E.H.R. Green Was Trusted by the "World's Richest Woman," Whose Close Friends Say She Was

Kind and Not Parsimonious. (1916, July 9). *The New York Times*. Retrieved June 28, 2014

Hetty Greens's Husband is Dead. (1902, March 2). *The New York Times*.

Hicks, J. (Ed.). (1988). *A Mystic River Anthology*. Wickford, Rhode Island: The Dutch Island Press.

Historians Corner. (n.d.). *The Sisson Stones*. Mystic River Historical Society.

Holy Trinity and C S Lewis. (n.d.). Retrieved October 1, 2014, from Holy Trinity Church, Headington Quarry, Oxford, England:: http://www.hthq.org.uk/holy-trinity-and-c-s-lewis.html

Hubbard, K., & Mathison, D. (1988, October 31). George Burns Writes a Final Loving Tribute to Gracie Allen. *People*, pp. 58-60. Retrieved from http://www.people.com/people/archive/article/0,,20100336,00.html

Hundreds in Tribute to Grandma Moses. (1961, December 15). Retrieved from The New York Times: ProQuest Historical Newspapers.

Hunt, J. (2014, August). What Now? Living with Purpose as a Senior Adult. *Mature Living*, p. 28.

In Memoriam: Drowned off Galveston Bar...Steamer City of Waco...Capt. Thomas Eldredge Wolfe...Inquest. (n.d.). *Retrieved from Mystic River Historical Society*.

Kallir, O. (1973). *Grandma Moses*. New York: Harrison House/Harry N. Abrams, Inc.

Katharine Graham 1917-2001. (2001, July 17). Retrieved from The Washington Post: http://www.washingtonpost.com/wp-dyn/content/article/2006/03/20/AR2006032000789.html

Katharine Graham: A Life Remembered. (2001, July 17). Retrieved from NPR: http://www.npr.org/news/specials/kgraham/010717.kgraham.html

Ketchum Jr., William C. (1996). *Grandma Moses: An American Original*. New York: Smithmark Publishers.

Kilpatrick, C. (1974, August 6). *Nixon Resigns*. Retrieved from The Washington Post: http://www.washingtonpost.com/wp-srv/national/longterm/watergate/articles/080974-3.htm

Kimball, C. (n.d.). *Anna Warner Bailey*. Retrieved October 18, 2014, from Anna Warner Bailey Chapter, National Society of Daughters of American Revolution: http://annawarnerbaileydar.org/pb/wp_6b4f8f03/wp_6b4f8f03.html

Kimball, C. W. (1990, October 18). The mystery of Abigail Hinman: Revolution Story. *The Day*, p. C7.

Kimball, C. W. (2002, January 17). Capt. Thomas E. Wolfe of Mystic lived life to the hilt. *The Day*, p. Retrieved from Mystic River Historical Socieity.

Kimball, C. W. (2007, July 4). Abby Day Slocomb: She Made a Difference. *The Day* . Retrieved from http://news.google.com/newspapers?nid=1915&dat=20070604&id=pbctAAAAIBAJ&sjid=J3MFAAAAIBAJ&pg=2690,838973

King Jr, M. L. (1963). *I Have A Dream Speech*. Retrieved April 1, 2016, from Huffington Post: http://www.huffingtonpost.com/2011/01/17/i-have-a-dream-speech-text_n_809993.html

King Jr., Martin Luther. (1968, April 3). *Martin Luther King Jr.'s Prophetic Last Speech: "I've Been to the Mountaintop"*. Retrieved from Youtube: https://www.youtube.com/watch?v=wzG3VMTGRVA

King, C. S. (1969). *My Life With Martin Luther King, Jr.* New York: Holt, Rinehart and Winston.

Lehrman, L. (2010, February 19). Martha Washington: The First Lady. *Connecticut Post*.

Lewis, C. S., 1961, Afterward by Chad Walsh. (1976). In *A Grief Observed*. New York: Bantam Books.

Life at Mount Vernon Before the Presidency. (2016, March 29). Retrieved from Martha Washington: A Life: http://marthawashington.us/exhibits/show/martha-washington--a-life/life-at-mt--vernon-before-the-

Life Book's. (2000). The Greatest Adventures of All Time. Time Inc. Home Entertainment.

Lovell, M. S. . (1989). *The Sound of Wings: The Life of Amelia Earhart*. New York: St. Martin's Press.

Mancini, J. (April 3, 2011). *The Connecticut State Flag; Go Girls! Abby Day Slocomb and Daughters of the*. Groton, Connecticut.

Mark Twain is Dead at 74. (1910, April 21). *The New York Times*. Retrieved from http://www.nytimes.com/learning/general/onthisday/big/0421.html

Marshall, B. T. (1922). *A modern history of New London County, Connecticut*. Lewis Historical Publishing Company. Retrieved from http://books.google.com/books?id=pAkWAAAAYAAJ&pg=PA226&dq=captain+charles+sisson&hl=en&sa=X&ei=53wMT8T5IqHq0gHLxrXlBQ&ved=0CDEQ6AEwAA#v=onepage&q=captain%20charles%20sisson&f=false

Mattioli, B. (2014, July 30). Park Supervisor, Gillette Castle State Park. (L. Saunders, Interviewer)

McKay, N. (2014, April 16). Previous owner 12 Mystic Ave, Mystic, CT . (J. A. Hicks, Interviewer)

McManus, M. M. (2012, July). *Researchers Searching For Amelia Earhart's Plane Wreckage Sail From Hawaii To Nikumaroro*. Retrieved August 2012, from Huffington Post: http://www.huffingtonpost.com/2012/07/03/amelia-earhart-search-hawaii-nikumaroro_n_1648117.html

Milton and Kitty: A Love Story. (n.d.). Retrieved March 29, 2016, from Milton Hershey School: http://www.mhskids.org/news-feed/milton-and-kitty-a-love-story-2/

Moore, Shirley McMillan. (2016, March 31). *Grandma Moses: My Life's History*. Retrieved from The Flyters Debut: http://theflytersdebut.com/blog/?p=35

Mrs. Chas. Sisson photograph. (n.d.). *Bradley Collection: 1992.034.0002*. Mystic, CT: Mystic River Historical Society.

Mystic River Historical Society. (1995). *Curbstones, Clapboards and Cupolas*. Mystic Rivers Historical Society. Retrieved from http://www.mystichistory.org/tours/curbstones_booklet.pdf

Mystic River Historical Society. (2004). *Images of America Mystic*. Arcadia Publishing.

Mystic River Historical Society. (n.d.). Mystic River Walking Adventure. Retrieved from www.mystichistory.org/MRHSTourGravelnobg_72dpi.pdf

Mystic River Historical Society. (n.d.). *Town of Groton, Connecticut, records transcribed by Carol W. Kimball*. Mystic, CT. Retrieved 2013

National Society Daughters of American Revolution. (n.d.). Mrs. Abby H. Day Slocomb. In *Lineage Book, NSDAR, Vol. 3*.

Neider, C. (Ed.). (1917). *The Autobiography of Mark Twain*. New York: Harper & Brothers.

New World Encyclopedia contributors. (April, 2015 14). *Martin Luther King, Jr*. Retrieved April 1, 2016, from New World Encyclopedia: http://www.newworldencyclopedia.org/entry/Martin_Luther_King,_Jr.

Pépin, J. (2015, June 3). French Chef, TV personality. (L. Saunders, Interviewer)

Permanent Exhibits. (n.d.). Retrieved from Bennington Museum: http://www.benningtonmuseum.org/whats-coming.html

Peterson, W. (2010, November 17). Mystic Historian. (L. Saunders, Interviewer)

Peterson, W. N. (1989). *"Mystic Built": Ships and Shipyards of the Mystic River, 1784-1919.* . Mystic : Mystic Seaport Museum.

Peterson, W. N. (1998). The Wartime Shipbuilding Boom at Mystic, Connecticut. In W. M. Benjamin W. Labaree, *American and the Sea: A Maritime History* (pp. 358-359). Mystic, CT: Mystic Seaport.

Potter. (1870, July,14). *Census. Groton, Connecticut, USA: Government*.

Powers, R. (2005). *Mark Twain: a life*. New York: Free Press.

Rash, N. (1994). History and Family: Daniel Huntington and the Patronage of Thomas Davis Day. *Archives of American Art Journal*, Vol. 34, No. 3 , 2-15.

Records transcribed by Carol W. Kimball. (n.d.). *12 West Mystic Avenue, Mystic, Connecticut*. Town of Groton, Connecticut: Mystic River Historical Society. Retrieved 2013

Richardson, A. D. (1865). *The Secret Service, the Field, the Dungeon, and the Escape*. Hartford, Connecticut: American Publishing Company. Retrieved April 2016, from https://archive.org/stream/secretservicefie5499rich#page/n7/mode/2up

Richest Woman in America. (2016, March 29). Retrieved from Mass Moments: http://www.massmoments.org/moment.cfm?mid=335

Roberts, C. (2004). *Founding Mothers: The Women Who Raised Our Nation*. New York: HarperCollins.

Roberts, C. (2008). *Ladies of Liberty: The Women Who Shaped Our Nation*. New York : HarperCollins Publishers, Inc.

Rockwell, N. (1994). *Willie Was Different*. Stockbridge, Massachussetts: Berkshire House Publishers.

Rose, A. S. (1899). *The Ninth New York Heavy Artillery*. Worcester, Mass.: Published By the Author.

Saunders, L. (2012, Revised June 21, 2015). *Mystic Seafarer's Trail*. Mystic, Connecticut: Createspace.

Saunders, L. (2014, July). Widow/er of History - Illustrator Norman Rockwell Finds Poetry—and a New Reason to Live. *Pathfinder: A Companion Guide to the Widow/er's Journey*. Retrieved from http://pathfindermag.com/read-online/2014-pathfinder-editions/07-2014-edition/64-widow-er-history

Saunders, L. (2014, Dec). Widow/er of History - Martha Washington - Two Times a Widow. *Pathfinder: A Companion Guide to the Widow/er's Journey*. Retrieved from http://pathfindermag.com/read-online/2014-pathfinder-editions/12-2014-edition/105-widow-er-history

Saunders, L. (2014, Sept). Widow/er of History - Mary Todd Lincoln the Widow. *Pathfinder: A Companion Guide to the Widow/er's Journey*. Retrieved from http://pathfindermag.com/read-online/2014-pathfinder-editions/09-2014-edition/71-widow-er-history

Saunders, L. (2014, Nov). Widow/er of History - The Love Story That Inspired Hershey's Kiss. *Pathfinder: A Companion Guide to the Widow/er's Journey*. Retrieved from http://pathfindermag.com/read-online/2014-pathfinder-editions/10-2014-edition/89-widow-er-history

Saunders, L. (2014, Aug). Widow/er of History - Two Sea Captains But Only One Widow's Walk. *Pathfinder: A Companion Guide to the Widow/er's Journey*. Retrieved from http://pathfindermag.com/read-online/2014-pathfinder-editions/08-2014-edition/35-widow-er-history

Saunders, L. (2015, May/June). Widow/er of History - Amelia Earhart's Widower, George Palmer Putnam - Moving On When There Is No Body. *Pathfinder: A Companion Guide to the Widow/er's Journey*. Retrieved from http://pathfindermag.com/read-online/2015-pathfinder-editions/05-2015-edition/211-widow-er-history

Saunders, L. (2015, Feb). Widow/er of History - C. S. Lewis, Author of the "Chronicles of Narnia" - Surprised by Joy, Love and Loss. *Pathfinder: A Companion Guide to the Widow/er's Journey*. Retrieved from http://pathfindermag.com/read-online/2015-pathfinder-editions/02-2015-edition/163-widow-er-history

Saunders, L. (2015, April). Widow/er of History - George Burns and Gracie Allen: The Show Must Go On. *Pathfinder: A Companion Guide to the Widow/er's Journey*. Retrieved from http://pathfindermag.com/read-online/2015-pathfinder-editions/04-2015-edition/194-widow-er-history

Saunders, L. (2015, Jan). Widow/er of History - Hetty Green Guinness World Record Holder: Greatest Miser "Witch of Wall Street". *Pathfinder: A Companion Guide to the Widow/er's Journey*. Retrieved from http://pathfindermag.com/read-online/2015-pathfinder-editions/01-2015-edition/131-widow-er-history

Saunders, L. (2015, Nov). Widow/er of History - Julia Child – Continued Recipe for Success After Widowhood. *Pathfinder: A Companion Guide to the Widow/er's Journey*. Retrieved from http://pathfindermag.com/read-online/2015-pathfinder-editions/11-2015-edition/265-widow-er-history

Saunders, L. (2015, Dec). Widow/er of History - King Henry VIII Married Six Wives, Outlived Four, Widowed How Many? . *Pathfinder: A Companion Guide to the Widow/er's Journey*. Retrieved from http://widowedpathfinder.us10.list-manage.com/track/click?u=e5e0c01fe47207c6015bafafe&id=6e79a989f1&e=de536243c5

Saunders, L. (2015, July/Aug). Widow/er of History - Sherlock Holmes, William Gillette and the One Woman. *Pathfinder: A Companion Guide to the Widow/er's Journey*. Retrieved from http://pathfindermag.com/read-online/2015-pathfinder-editions/07-2015-edition/227-widow-er-history

Saunders, L. (2015, Sept/Oct). Widow/er of History - Widow Grandma Moses Begins Painting In Her Late 70s. *Pathfinder: A Companion*

Guide to the Widow/er's Journey. Retrieved from http://pathfindermag.com/read-online/2015-pathfinder-editions/09-2015-edition/246-widow-er-history

Saunders, L. (2015, March). Widow/er of History - Widowed Sea Captain Finds Wife, Mother for His Seven Children, and "The Sound of Music". *Pathfinder: A Companion Guide to the Widow/er's Journey.* Retrieved from http://pathfindermag.com/index.php/read-online/2015-pathfinder-editions/03-2015-edition/182-widow-er-history

Saunders, L. (2016, Jan/Feb). Widow/er of History - Coretta Scott King Marched On. *Pathfinder: A Companion Guide to the Widow/er's Journey.* Retrieved from http://pathfindermag.com/read-online/2016-pathfinder-editions/01-2016-edition/303-widow-er-history

Saunders, L. (2016, March/April). Widow/er of History - Mark Twain "Adopts" Granddaughters. *Pathfinder: A Companion Guide to the Widow/er's Journey.* Retrieved from http://pathfindermag.com/read-online/2016-pathfinder-editions/03-2016-edition/315-widow-er-history

Sayer, G. (1988). *Jack, C. S. Lewis and His Times.* Harper & Row, Publishers, San Francisco.

Schaefer, Richard G; Connecticut State Historic Preservation Office. (2004). *His beloved Aunt Polly : Aunt Polly Archaeological Preserve, East Haddam, Connecticut.* Westport, CT : Historical Perspectives.

School History. (n.d.). Retrieved April 16, 2016, from Milton Hershey School: http://www.mhskids.org/about/school-history/

Seventy Years Rest Lightly on Mrs. Hetty Green: Tuesday Fortnight the Richest Woman in America Will Be Threescore and Ten --- Her Optimistic Outlook Upon Life --- Foundation and Growth of Her Great Fortune. (1905, November 5). *The New York Times.*

Shapiro, L. (2007). *Julia Child.* New York: Viking Group.

Shippen, Katherine B.; Wallace, Paul A.W. (1959). *Milton S. Hershey.* Amereon House.

Sisson, C. C. (1863-1884). Sisson Family Bible. Charles C. Sisson Papers. Mystic , Connecticut, U.S.A.: Retrieved From G. W. Blunt White Library, Mystic Seaport. (n.d.).

Sisson, C. C. (1876). Charles C. Sisson Journal. Charles C. Sisson Papers (Coll. 114, Volume 6). Mystic , Connecticut , U.S.A.: Retrieved from G. W. Blunt White Library, Mystic Seaport. (n.d.).

Slack, C. (2004). *Slack, CHetty: The Genius and Madness of America's First Female Tycoon.* New York: HarperCollins.

Slocomb, A. D. (1914, November 26). Time Capsule Letter. Zurich, Switzerland: Anna Warner Bailey Chapter, National Society of

Daughters of the American Revolution. Retrieved September 6, 2014

Smith, L. B. (1971). *Henry VIII: The Mask of Royalty.* Boston: Houghton Mifflin Company .

Smith, S. (2009, January 10). Milton Hershey's link to Titanic highlights exhibit. *The Patriot-News.*

Solomon, D. (2013). *American Mirror: the life and art of Norman Rockwell.* New York: Farrar, Straus and Giroux.

Souza, M. (2014, September 18). Time capsule from 1914 a window into WWI. *Mystic River Press, the Westerly Sun.* Retrieved from http://www.mysticriverpress.com/news/latestnews/4488762-129/time-capsule-from-1914-a-window-into-wwi.html

Spach, C. (1915, March 1). Special Commissioner. *Letter.* St. Gall, Switzerland: 02.AWB.1.393.1.

Spitz, B. (2012). *Dearie: The Remarkable Life of Julia Child.* New York:: A.A. Knopf.

Stranks, M. (2014, October 1). C.S. Lewis Guide, Holy Trinity Church, Headington Quarry, Oxford, England. (L. Saunders, Interviewer)

The 1790s: Retirement at Mount Vernon. (n.d.). Retrieved March 29, 2016, from Martha Washington: A Life: http://marthawashington.us/exhibits/show/martha-washington--a-life/the-1790s/retirement

THE BURNED STEAMER: MORE ACCOUNTS OF THE DISASTER. THE DESTRUCTION OF THE CITY OF WACO AT GALVESTON HOPELESS SEARCH FOR THE PASSENGERS AND CREW. CRUISE OF THE BUCKTHORN. FACTS AND CONCLUSIONS. LOCAL COMPANIES. CAPT. THOMAS WOLFE'S BODY TO BE SENT TO CONN. (1875, November 15). *The New York Times.*

The Burning of the Waco. (1875, Nov 11). *New York Times* .

THE CITY OF WACO.; THE BODY OF CAPT. WOLFE, THE GALVESTON PILOT, RECOVERED NO HOPE THAT ANY OF THOSE ON BOARD ESCAPED. (1875, November 14). *The New York Times.*

The Death of George Washington. (n.d.). Retrieved March 29, 2016, from George Washington's Mount Vernon: http://www.mountvernon.org/digital-encyclopedia/article/the-death-of-george-washington/

The Earhart Project. (n.d.). Retrieved September 16, 2012, from The International Group for Historic Aircraft Recovery (TIGHAR): http://tighar.org/Projects/Earhart/Archives/Research/Bulletins/63_DebrisField/63_DebrisField.htm

The International Group for Historical Aircraft Recovery. (n.d.). Retrieved August 2012, from TIGHAR: http://tighar.org/

The Loss of the Waco Two hundred Cases of Oil Found Floating. (1875, November 25). *New York Times*.

The Man. (n.d.). Retrieved November 20, 2015, from Mark Twain House and Museum: http://marktwainhouse.org/man/biography_main.php

The Twilight Years:The Deaths of George and Martha Washington. (n.d.). Retrieved April 16, 2016, from Martha Washington: http://marthawashington.us/exhibits/show/martha-washington--a-life/the-twilight-years/deaths

Thompson, C. W. (1930, April 27). The Strange Case of Hetty Green. *The New York Times*.

Trapp, M. A. (1949). *The Story of the Trapp Family Singers*. New York: Dell Publishing Co., Inc.

Turner, A. (2005, July 24). Historians explore-tragedy of the City of Waco. *Houston Chronical*.

Turner, Justin G. and Linda L. (1972). *Mary Todd Lincoln*. New York: Alfred A. Knopf.

Vaudeville. (n.d.). Retrieved 2014, from Merriam-Webster: http://www.merriam-webster.com/dictionary/vaudeville

Von Trapp Story. (n.d.). Retrieved October 22, 2014, from Trapp Family Lodge: http://www.trappfamily.com/story

Waterman, C. (2010). *Landmarks You Must Visit In Southeast Connecticut*. Mystic, Connecticut: Matthew Goldman aka Constant Waterman.

Weir, A. (2001). *Henry VIII: The King and His Court*. New York: Ballantine Books.

Who Served Here? Martha Washington. (n.d.). Retrieved April 16, 2016, from Historic Valley Forge: http://www.ushistory.org/valleyforge/served/martha.html

Wilbur, D. F. (1915, April 3). Consul-General of the United States of America. *Letter*. Zurich, Switzerland: 02-AWB.1.393.1.

Wise, R. (Director). (1965). *The Sound of Music* [Motion Picture].

Wolfe, F. (1875, Nov 18). Donations to the Family of the Late Capt. Wolfe. *Galveston Daily News*.

Wolfe, T. E. (1863, 1864). Letters, 1863-1865, from Thomas E. Wolfe. *All but one letter is written to his wife from Castle Thunder Prison*. Mystic, Connecticut: Retrieved From G. W. Blunt White Library, Mystic Seaport.

Young, S. (1970, November 11). Amelia Earhart Made News in Noank. *The Day--Retrieved from Noank Historical Society, Inc., Research Files*, p. 40.

Zecher, H. (2011). *William Gillette, America's Sherlock Holmes*. Xlibris Corporation.

Zecher, H. (n.d.). *William Gillette*. Retrieved April 16, 2016, from
    HenryZecher.com: http://www.henryzecher.com/gillettebio.htm
Zolotow, M. (1980). "Oh God!" It's George Burns! *Readers Digest*, pp. 209-
    214.

[1] Erickson, 1980, p.332

[2] Henry VIII, 2008

[3] Erickson, 1980, p.332, 333

[4] Henry VIII, 2008

[5] Roberts, C., 2004, *Founding Mothers: The Women Who Raised Our Nation*, p.86)

[6] Life at Mount Vernon Before the Presidency, 2016

[7] Roberts, C., 2004, *Founding Mothers: The Women Who Raised Our Nation*, p.235

[8] Roberts, C., 2004, *Founding Mothers: The Women Who Raised Our Nation*, p.238

[9] The 1790s: Retirement at Mount Vernon, n.d.

[10] The Death of George Washington, n.d.

[11] Turner, Justin G. and Linda L., 1972, pp. 284, 285

[12] Turner, Justin G. and Linda L., 1972, p. 222

[13] Explore Lincoln: Learn the Story, p. 18

[14] Roe, 1899, pp. 241, 242

[15] Explore Lincoln: Learn the Story, p. 23

[16] Explore Lincoln: Learn the Story, p. 24

[17] Explore Lincoln: Learn the Story, p. 24

[18] Explore Lincoln: Learn the Story, p. 24

[19] Fleischner, 2003, p. 290

[20] Turner, Justin G. and Linda L., 1972, p. 230

[21] Turner, Justin G. and Linda L., 1972, p. 258

[22] Turner, Justin G. and Linda L., 1972, p. 268

[23] Fleischner, 2003, p. 321

[24] Powers, 2005, p. 617

[25] Gaffney, 2008

[26] Gaffney, 2008

[27] Hicks, 1988, p. 175

[28] Powers, 2005, p.616

[29] Burns, 2001

[30] Powers, 2005, p.615

[31] Powers, 2005, p.616

[32] Neider, 1917, p.343

[33] Gaffney, 2008

[34] Powers, 2005, p.619

[35] Gaffney, 2008

[36] Gaffney, 2008

[37] Gaffney, 2008

[38] Powers, 2005, p.619

[39] Neider, 1917, p.372

[40] Neider, 1917, p. 378

[41] Neider, 1917, p. 379

[42] Slack, C., 2004, *Hetty: The Genius and Madness of America's First Female* Tycoon, p.xi

[43] Slack, C., 2004, Hetty: *The Genius and Madness of America's First Female Tycoon*, p.3

[44] "The Strange Case of Hetty Green," The *New York Times*, Apr. 27, 1930

[45] HETTY GREEN DIES, 1916

[46] Wolfe T. E., 1863, 1864

[47] Richardson, 1865, p. 471

[48] Richardson, 1865, p.463

[49] The Burning of the Waco, 1875

[50] THE BURNED STEAMER: MORE ACCOUNTS OF THE DISASTER. THE DESTRUCTION OF THE CITY OF WACO AT GALVESTON HOPELESS SEARCH FOR THE PASSENGERS AND CREW. CRUISE OF THE BUCKTHORN. FACTS AND CONCLUSIONS. LOCAL COMPANIES. CAPT. THOMAS WOLFE'S BODY TO BE SENT TO CONN, 1875, Nov 15, *New York Times*

[51] THE BURNED STEAMER: MORE ACCOUNTS OF THE DISASTER. THE DESTRUCTION OF THE CITY OF WACO AT GALVESTON HOPELESS SEARCH FOR THE PASSENGERS AND CREW. CRUISE OF THE BUCKTHORN. FACTS AND CONCLUSIONS. LOCAL COMPANIES. CAPT. THOMAS WOLFE'S BODY TO BE SENT TO CONN, 1875, Nov 15, *New York Times*

[52] In Memoriam: Drowned off Galveston Bar...Steamer City of Waco...Capt. Thomas Eldredge Wolfe...Inquest

[53] Wolfe, F., 1875

[54] Charles C. Sisson Papers (Coll. 114, Volume 6, pg 293

[55] Charles C. Sisson Papers (Coll. 114, Volume 6, pg 294

[56] Charles C. Sisson Papers (Coll. 114, Volume 6, pg 303

[57] Charles C. Sisson Papers (Coll. 114, Volume 6, pg 309

[58] Records transcribed by Carol W. Kimball

[59] His Beloved Aunt Polly, p. 3

[60] Zecher, p. 181

[61] Zecher, p. 182

[62] Zecher, p. 181

[63] His Beloved Aunt Polly, 2004, p. 5

[64] Zecher, 2011, p. 386

[65] His Beloved Aunt Polly, 2004, p. 9

[66] Zecher, 2001, p. 7

[67] Lovell, 1989, p. 154

[68] Dorothy Putnam

[69] Long & Long, 1999, p. 37
[70] AMELIA EARHART BIOGRAPHICAL SKETCH
[71] Butler, 1999, p. 238
[72] Chick, 1989, p. 40
[73] Mill, 1976
[74] Mill, 1976
[75] Earhart, Letter, 1931 Feb. 7, Noank, Conn., to GPP (draft), 1931
[76] Mill, 1976
[77] Mill, 1976
[78] AMELIA EARHART WEDS G.P. PUTNAM, 1931
[79] Mill, 1976
[80] Chick, 1989
[81] Mill, 1976
[82] Mary Virginia Goodman, circa 1971
[83] AMELIA EARHART WEDS G.P. PUTNAM, 1931
[84] Robert P. Anderson, Jr., November 17, 2010
[85] AMELIA EARHART BIOGRAPHICAL SKETCH
[86] Life Book's, 2000, p. 147
[87] Lovell, 1989, p. 197
[88] Life Book's, 2000, p. 148
[89] Lovell, 1989, p. 293
[90] AMELIA EARHART BIOGRAPHICAL SKETCH
[91] Wilson, 1982
[92] Lovell, 1989, p. 301
[93] Lovell, 1989, p. 304
[94] Lovell, 1989, p. 315
[95] Fagin, 1979
[96] McManus, 2012
[97] Shippen and Wallace, 1959, p. 94
[98] Shippen and Wallace, 1959, p. 95
[99] Shippen and Wallace, 1959, p.100
[100] Milton and Kitty: A Love Story, n.d.
[101] Shippen and Wallace, 1959, p. 138
[102] Shippen and Wallace, 1959, p. 137
[103] Hershey, Catherine Sweeney. n.d.
[104] Shippen and Wallace, 1959, p. 179
[105] Grandma Moses is Dead at 101: Primitive Artist 'Just wore out', 1961
[106] Hunt, 2014, p.28
[107] Kallir, 1973, p.19
[108] Kallir, 1973, p.25

[109] Kallir, 1973, p. 38

[110] Grandma Moses is Dead at 101: Primitive Artist 'Just wore out', 1961

[111] Kallir, 1973, p. 45

[112] Moore, Shirley McMillan, 2016

[113] Kallir, 1973, p. 122

[114] Kallir, 1973, p. 173-175

[115] Lewis, 1961, p. 141

[116] Lewis, 1961, p. 147

[117] Lewis, 1961, p. 18

[118] Lewis, 1961, p. 88

[119] Lewis, 1961, p.8

[120] Lewis, 1961, p. 147

[121] Lewis, 1961, p.89

[122] Lewis, 1961, p.5

[123] Solomon, *American Mirror: The Life and Art of Normal Rockwell*, 2013, p. 356

[124] Trapp, 1949, *The Story of the Trapp Family Singers*, p.11

[125] Trapp, 1949, *The Story of the Trapp Family Singers*, p.13

[126] Trapp, 1949, *The Story of the Trapp Family Singers*, p.31

[127] Trapp, 1949, *The Story of the Trapp Family Singers*, p.117

[128] Trapp, 1949, *The Story of the Trapp Family Singers*, p.119

[129] Trapp, 1949, *The Story of the Trapp Family Singers*, p.120

[130] Trapp, 1949, *The Story of the Trapp Family Singers*, p.141

[131] Trapp, 1949, *The Story of the Trapp Family Singers*, p.252

[132] Trapp, 1949, *The Story of the Trapp Family Singers*, p.331

[133] Trapp, 1949, *The Story of the Trapp Family Singers*, p.345

[134] Gottfriend, 1996, p. 12

[135] Burns G. , 1988, p.303

[136] Burns G. , 1988, dust jacket

[137] Burns G. , 1988, p.16

[138] Burns G. , 1988, p. 13

[139] Gottfriend, 1996, p. 49

[140] Gottfriend, 1996, p.56

[141] Gottfriend, 1996, p.60

[142] Burns G., 1988, p.65

[143] Burns G., 1988, p.68

[144] Gottfriend, 1996, p.81

[145] Hubbard & Mathison, 1988

[146] Burns G. , 1988, p.303

[147] Burns G., 1988, p. 306

[148] Burns G. , 1988, p. 306, 307

[149] Zolotow, 1980, p.210

[150] Zolotow, 1980, p.214

[151] Zolotow, 1980, p.214

[152] Hubbard & Mathison, 1988

[153] Graham, *Katherine Graham,* 1999, p. 333

[154] Graham, *Personal History,* 1997, p. 337

[155] Graham, *Personal History,* 1997, p. 339

[156] Graham, *Personal History,* 1997, p. 340

[157] Graham, *Personal History,* 1997, p. 340

[158] Graham, *Katherine Graham,* 1999, p. 337

[159] Graham, *Personal History,* 1997, p. 341

[160] Graham, *Katherine Graham,* 1999, pp. 337, 338

[161] Graham, *Personal History,* 1997, p. 450

[162] Graham, *Katherine Graham,* 1999, p. 337

[163] Kilpatrick, 1974

[164] Graham, *Katherine Graham's Washington,* 2002, p. 4

[165] Graham, *Katherine Graham,* 1999, p. 338

[166] Graham, *Katherine Graham,* 1999, p. 336

[167] Graham, *Katherine Graham's Washington,* 2002, p. 5

[168] BERGER, 2001

[169] Chef Jacques Pépin: Cooking for Widow/ers, Dr. Joanne Z. Moore, Pathfinder, Lisa Saunders Show , 2015, https://www.youtube.com/watch?v=WB891yRO90A

[170] Spitz, 2012, *Dearie: The Remarkable Life of Julia Child,* p. 130

[171] Spitz, 2012, *Dearie: The Remarkable Life of Julia Child,* p. 141

[172] Spitz, 2012, *Dearie: The Remarkable Life of Julia Child,* p. 181

[173] Spitz, 2012, *Dearie: The Remarkable Life of Julia Child,* p.181

[174] Fitch, 1977, *Appetite for Life: The Biography of Julia Child,* p. 484

[175] Pépin, 2015

[176] Child, Julia with Prud'homme, Alex, 2006, *My Life in France,* p. x

[177] Child, Julia with Prud'homme, Alex, 2006, *My Life in France,* p.3, 5

[178] Child, Julia with Prud'homme, Alex, 2006, *My Life in France,* p.3

[179] Child, Julia with Prud'homme, Alex, 2006, *My Life in France,* p.8

[180] King Jr., 1963

[181] King Jr., Martin Luther, 1968

[182] King, C., 1969, p.318

[183] King, C., 1969, p.320

[184] King, C., 1969, p.328

[185] King, C., 1969, p.329

[186] King, C., 1969, p.55

[187] Martin Luther King, Jr., n.d.—the New World Encyclopedia

[188] King, C., 1969, p.329

[189] Biography.com Editors, n.d. Corette Scott King

[190] AAUW Coretta Scott King Fellows: Scholars and Women of Action, n.d.

[191] Abby Day Slocomb's house, with the current address of 241 Monument Street, was the site of first Anna Warner Bailey Chapter meeting held on Sept. 13, 1893 with 16 local ladies.

[192] Kimball C. W., Abby Day Slocomb: She Made a Difference, 2007

[193] Mancini, April 3, 2011

[194] Anna Warner Bailey and her husband, Elijah Bailey, a veteran of the Battle of Groton Heights, had no children and became inn keepers. Anna outlived Elijah and died in her 90s when a spark from the fireplace landed on her clothes while she slept. The home/inn she died in is currently owned by the City of Groton and can be seen at 108 Thames Street, Groton, Connecticut.

[195] Souza, 2014

[196] Spach, C. (1915, March 1). Special Commissioner. Letter. St. Gall, Switzerland: 02.AWB.1.393.1.

[197] Letter transcribed by Robert Purinton, Amateur Historian/Genealogist (2014, September 6.

[198] Transcribed: IS THE KAISER MAD?

Petrograd, Thursday.—the Russian papers are more and more inclined to take the view that Emperor William is insane. They cite to-day his proclamation to the Poles in Czenstochow, in which he referred to a miraculous ringing of the bells at the Sviatogorosky monastery and declared that it denoted his decision to make war on Russia, restore sacred possessions of Poland and unite Poland to Germany, the most cultured country. The Kaiser added: "I had a wondrous dream. The Virgin appeared to me and entrusted me with the rescue of her sacred habitation. She gazed at me tearfully, and I went forth to execute her holy will."

The Kaiser called on the Poles to meet with German troops as their brothers and saviors. Those who were with him, he said, would be amply rewarded, while those who were against him would perish. He concluded with these words: "With me are God and the Holy Virgin, who have drawn the German sword in aid of Poland."—Reuter.

[199] Rash, 1994

[200] The portrait, completed in 1856, was donated by the family to the Lyman Allyn Art Museum in New London, Connecticut. It made the cover of the 2006 book, *Revolutionary Mothers: Women in the Struggle for America's Independence*, by Carol Berkin.

www.ingramcontent.com/pod-product-compliance
Lightning Source LLC
Chambersburg PA
CBHW031319040426
42443CB00005B/146